ARCHITECTURE SOURCE BOOK

Sagrada Familia,
Barcelona, Spain *(begun*
1884). Antonio Gaudi.

ARCHITECTURE SOURCE BOOK

VERNON GIBBERD

THE WELLFLEET PRESS
WELLFLEET

A QUARTO BOOK

Published by Wellfleet Press
110 Enterprise Avenue
Secaucus, New Jersey 07094

Copyright © 1988 Quarto Publishing plc

ISBN 1 55521 273 5

This book was designed and produced by
Quarto Publishing plc
The Old Brewery, 6 Blundell Street
London N7 9BH

Project Editor
Charyn Jones
Art Editor
Neville Graham

Consultant
Trewin Copplestone

Senior Editor
Kate Kirby

Art Director
Moira Clinch
Editorial Director
Carolyn King

Special thanks to
Patrizio Semproni, Beverley Pattison

Typeset by Ampersand Typesetters, Bournemouth
Manufactured in Hong Kong by Regent Publishing Services Ltd
Printed in Hong Kong by South Sea Int'l Press Ltd.

**Hong Kong Shanghai
Bank, Hong Kong** (1981-85).
Foster Associates.

CONTENTS

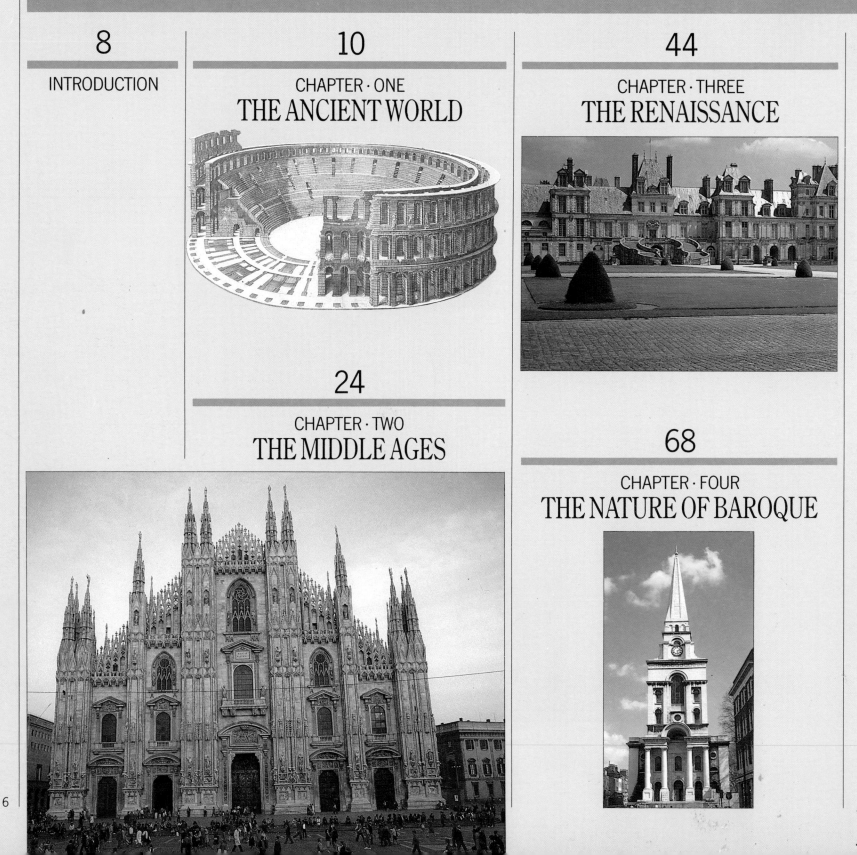

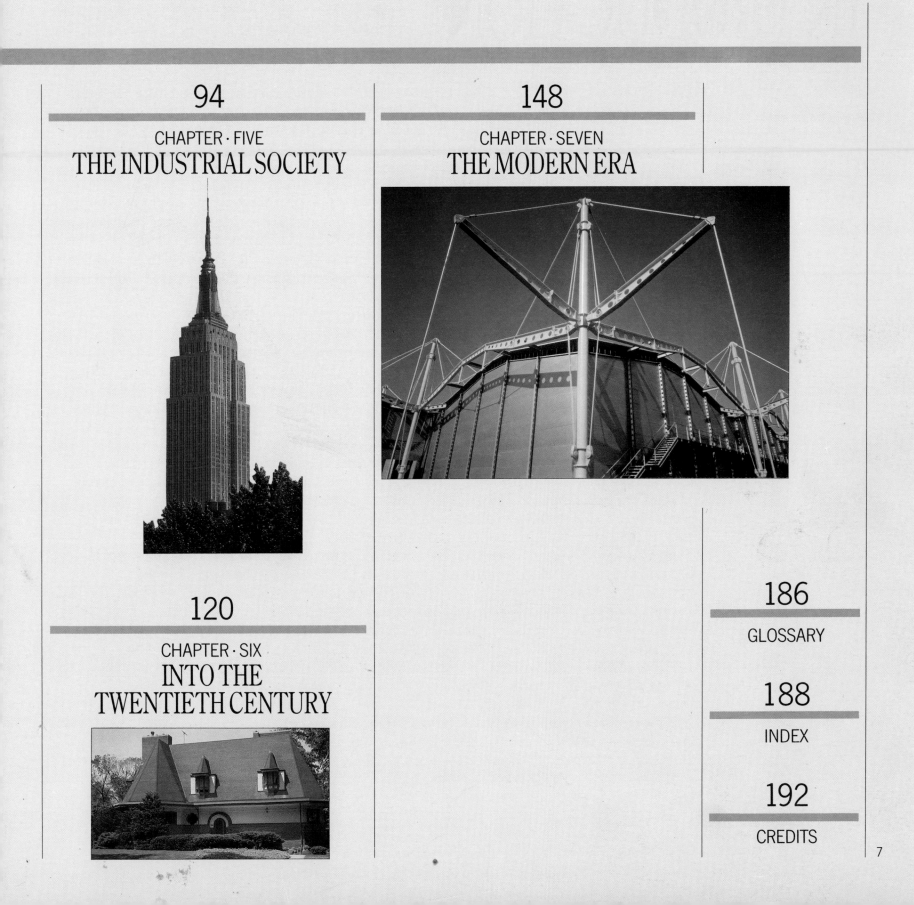

INTRODUCTION

The aim of this book is not to attempt a comprehensive survey of world architecture but to try and place the buildings of this century in the context of Western cultural history. Sadly, whole continents have had to be left out; for example the contributions of China, Japan, India and South America are neglected, not because they are second rate or unimportant, but because they had no direct bearing on the origins of the architecture which first emerged in countries around the Mediterranean in the centuries before Christ, spreading gradually across Europe and, in due course, influencing the entire world.

I have found it both a rewarding and humbling experience to be asked to reassess, for the first time since student days, the entire history of architecture from the time of the Pharaohs: rewarding because of the pleasure of greeting old favorites, and humbling to find so many buildings that I had forgotten or dismissed as derivative or outside some mainstream movement judged at the time to be important or historically inevitable.

Experience widens the frontiers of our enjoyment but at the same time deepens the sadness at mediocrity and impatience with self-important theories. The exclusivity of much of the polemics of the puritan years of the Modern Movement now seems irrelevant, and if our present climate of *laisser faire* has, as a direct result, led to the absence of a recognized and identifiable style, then at least we are spared the tedium of propaganda. Not that architects have stopped promoting and justifying their work in print, merely that nobody takes them too seriously any longer in a society where a hundred other voices are making alternative claims.

The same is evident in the other arts, and in the more ephemeral fields of graphics, fashion and interior decoration the manifestations are even more transient and exaggerated. Society has yet to come to terms with the twentieth century and with the full implications of post industrialism. Many of the brightest intellects have reacted enthusiastically to the challenge, others, equally persuasive, try to salvage from the past an approach to architecture which can be translated by modern means.

There is one factor which unites all buildings erected before the middle of the last century. Every component was either made or shaped by human beings, and its character thereby ineradicably conditioned by the skill or limitations of the craftsman. This gave architecture its peculiar nature – its grain – an elusive characteristic largely lost in modern technology. Now that we live in an age of mass industrial manufacture, we must come to terms with its often uncomfortable aesthetic. A standard door is just that – as like its neighbor as two ballpoint pens.

How successful the past century has been in reconciling this revolution must be left to the reader to judge. What I hope will become clear is that the architecture of any age is the product of its technology, refined by detailing, decoration and attention to proportion. In ancient Greece it was the perfection of the post and lintel, later expanded by the more extrovert and energetic Romans. When their empire declined, the Byzantine world explored and developed the dome in the service of early Christianity. This style returned to Europe to develop into Romanesque, which in turn flowered into Gothic when stone technology was exploited to its structural limits to provide the great cathedrals. The Renaissance restored intellectual order into architecture and remained the guiding spirit until the Industrial Revolution introduced new materials demanding new structural solutions.

We now live in a restless and eclectic age. The proliferation of printed and recorded information is so comprehensive that we can ransack the whole of history for inspiration, and this easy option may be one of the reasons for our apparent failure to produce an accepted style today, at any rate as this term would have been understood in the past. Coupled with this failure is our lack of creative self-confidence and uncertainty about the future.

The insistence on experiment, creative licence and change at all costs may prove to be both our salvation and undoing. The increasing world birthrate demands vast building programs merely to provide enough housing and places of work for exploding populations. For some the prospect is so uninviting that a retreat into an imagined past seems an attractive alternative, but the conditions of earlier centuries, with their cross currents of grandeur and squalor, can neither be recalled nor recreated.

However preferable our new social order may be, the attendant problems over standardization and urban conformity present new difficulties as yet dimly recognized. What I hope this brisk survey may do is show that, with energy and imagination, our architectural future may not of necessity be wholly bleak, and if this book succeeds in stimulating an enthusiasm for the buildings of the past, coupled with concern for those being put up today, then it will have been worthwhile. If at the same time it can persuade the reader that no one style is necessarily "correct" at the expense of another, and that good architecture can be enjoyed from every decade, then it will have doubly achieved its purpose.

Vernon Gibberd

CHAPTER ONE

THE ANCIENT WORLD

THE CLASSICAL ORDERS

9

CHAPTER ONE
THE ANCIENT WORLD

THE CLASSICAL ORDERS

INTRODUCTION

The distinction between architecture as opposed to mere building is hard to define, perhaps easier to recognize. No doubt many of the humbler buildings of early times, structures long since destroyed, displayed much technological ingenuity and attractive decoration, but, like their counterparts in primitive societies today, their status as architecture or building must remain a matter of personal choice. The twin threads of abstract design and structural experiment act and interact in buildings of all epochs, sometimes in harmony, at other times one taking precedence for a period over the other.

The earliest buildings that have survived, in the Middle East and particularly in Egypt, are mostly stone-built palaces and temples, structurally conservative but massively monumental, even oppressive. Their cost in human labor can only be imagined with a shudder: indeed how the common people and slaves lived must be left to the imagination or glimpsed in the cartoon-like images of wall paintings and ancient reliefs.

Architecture is only possible among settled communities no longer on the move and relatively untroubled by persistent wars. It is among settled agrarian communities

Stonehenge, Wiltshire, England *(2200-1300 BC). An intriguing monument to the ancient world. The axis is aligned with the rising sun on the longest day of the year in the northern hemisphere (21st June).*

therefore that we find nurseries of the arts, and when such conditions are fortified by successful foreign trade, such as in Egypt and Greece, then the architectural results can be dramatic.

Ancient Egypt

Egyptian civilization prospered from about 3000 BC until its gradual amalgamation into the Greek and then the Roman Empires. Until AD 100, Egyptian architecture was highly sophisticated but static – an architecture of monuments. The ruling kings, the Pharoahs, were regarded as god-kings: after death they spent unspecified years in a kind of purgatory, during which their souls inhabited other creatures, to return eventually as fully fledged divinities. To aid this happy metamorphosis, preparations in the form of funerary furnishings were provided in their tombs, which were concealed in the depths of colossal stone monuments, of which the pyramids are the most familiar.

Egyptian temples, unlike those of Greece or the later Christian churches, were entirely exclusive, designed for the god-king only and his or her high priests. The ordinary

11

citizens had no right of entry nor held any hopes of personal immortality. The mathematical accuracy of these constructions is staggering: the four sides of the great pyramid at Giza (c 2600-2500 BC) are equal to within fractions of an inch and the angle of approximately 52° was maintained in the building up, one on another, of some two million blocks of stone, each having been floated down the Nile from Upper Egypt.

All Egyptian building is essentially post and lintel, like Stonehenge or children's building blocks. By its molecular structure, stone is stronger as a post than as a beam, so the column spacing in the temples is necessarily close and claustrophobic. The columns themselves are interesting. It seems their shape derived from simple buildings, where bundles of reeds (wood was scarce) were bound together for greater strength as columns. Where the top of these took the weight of lintels above, a bulge formed, creating a capital, a feature which was to become of great importance in classical architecture.

The Greek Influence

Greek architecture is the most important and influential in Western history. Reaching a peak between 400-300 BC, it was developed, some would say vulgarized, by the Romans and then absorbed into the Byzantine.

It is a relief to turn to Greek architecture. The contrast in freedom and sanity after the Egyptian style is evident in all their buildings. This architecture too appears to have developed from wooden buildings; a translation, as it were, of carpentry technology into stone. The familiar triangular pediment evolved in the gable end of a pitched roof and the decorative elements of the frieze mimicked the joints and pegs of wooden joinery.

Pyramids, Cairo, Egypt
(c 3000 BC). The most familiar burial chambers of the Pharaohs of Egypt. Mathematically exact, they remain today a monument to the back-breaking task of bringing materials great distances and constructing such enduring monuments.

Reborn in fifteenth-century Italy, the Greeks have continued to inspire and influence architecture ever since, even today, surviving the mannerisms of "pop" experiments. It is, beneath its highly cerebral aesthetic, essentially a practical way of building in which decoration and sculpture are impeccably subordinated to the structure and function.

The Classical Orders

The orders of Greek architecture are important. These are what might be loosely called the three different styles of Greek architecture, known as the Doric, Ionic and Corinthian. However, they are something more than mere style, more of a formal discipline with its own rules of decoration, moulding and proportion to which each building in its entirety is subjected. It was simply not done, for instance, to put a Doric pediment on top of Ionic columns.

The earliest and most forthright order is Doric. The column is stubby, simply fluted with a plain capital. There is no base; the column stands square on the top platform of steps. The Dorians were intruders from the North and they drove the indigenous inhabitants to the coasts and islands. These were the less warlike Ionians, whose order is graceful and more decorated, instantly recognizable by the spiral volutes of its capitals. The third order is Corinthian, the tallest in proportion, with a carved capital incorporating stylized forms of the acanthus leaf.

As Greek architecture presents the peak of pure abstract design, then its greatest single masterpiece was the Parthenon, built, or rather rebuilt after destruction by the Persians, in about 440 BC. This temple, which housed the golden statue of the virgin Athena, is the dominant

building of the Acropolis, a group of temples built on a hill outside Athens. The sophistication of its geometry is legendary. The columns are bowed outwards slightly to avoid the impression of instability. Likewise the outer columns incline inwards, so gently that it has been calculated that their projected meeting point would be a mile above the temple. There is barely a straight line anywhere. Down below was the Agora, a meeting place of markets, shops, public buildings and small temples. Here Pericles spoke and Plato, Aristotle and Socrates wandered and talked, and presided over the birth of Western culture. Here was a chance, provided you were not a woman or a slave, to participate in the first open university.

Below the Acropolis, on the other side from the Agora, was built the theater of Dionysius which seated 30,000. Although the Greeks, like the Egyptians, were not structurally innovative, their technology was nevertheless astonishing, and the words of the actors and chorus could be heard from every seat, although there was no roof and probably only a light wooden structure behind the stage to reflect sound back at the audience.

The Roman Empire

Greek architecture spread along the sea route of the Mediterranean and temples are found in Sicily and Southern Italy. But the younger empire of Rome was by now expanding through sheer military and strategic energy and genius. Having absorbed the nearby Etruscans, whose architectural technology they took over,

Funeral Temple, Deir el Bahari, Egypt (1570-1314 BC). The restored tomb of Queen Hatshepsut with its many columns. Giant ramps connect the levels. This funeral monument was constructed in the New Kingdom period after a time of fairly minor building.

the small state of Rome quickly overran the whole of Italy. Sicily and North Africa followed and by the time of Julius Caesar, the Roman Empire stretched from Northumberland to Egypt, from Spain to Mesopotamia.

Their architecture reflects the extraordinary engineering inventiveness and public self-esteem and aggrandizement of the new empire. The Roman Forum was very different from the more cultivated Agora: it was an arena for public spectacle and games and contests of all kinds. Public buildings, thermal baths and stadia took precedence over temples, the Romans taking their religion more lightly than the Greeks – the most important deities being, in any case, household divinities. The Romans took religion, like architecture, from the Greeks but recast both to suit an extrovert and materialistic way of life. Little wonder that they favored the Corinthian order, with all its possibilities for elaboration and display.

Of their spectacular engineering skill, much has survived. The Romans were the first to lay down roads across Europe. Roads needed bridges, sometimes viaducts. They brought water in high aqueducts from the hills into Rome. The first large domed building, the Pantheon, was built. As the empire failed, when the huge territories could no longer be defended from barbarians from the North, their democracy and technology withered too. In AD 324, the Christian Emperor Constantine moved East and made his seat in modern day Istanbul.

GREEK ORDERS

1

2

1/2. Palace of Minos, Knossos, Crete (3000-2000 BC). A section of the restored palace of the kings of Minos, where royal apartments were built around a huge central court. What has survived in frescoes and artefacts reveals a highly organized early civilization.

The use of bold color in Minoan architecture continued through into Greek times. These white ruins were originally brightly decorated. Detail shows part of the staircase.

3. Treasury of Atreus at Mycenae, Greece (1400 BC). A citadel within a hillside, this view shows the entrance to a huge beehive-domed (tholos) funeral chamber of stone.

3

4. Olympia, Greece
(450 BC). Entrance to the stadium, site of the first Olympic Games. Greek columns were made up of drums so meticulously constructed that they fitted together without the need of mortar. Central dowels of wood or iron were used to keep them in position.

4

5

5. Temple of Zeus, Selinunte, Sicily *(540 BC). Detail of Doric capitals shows the simple concave fluting which lends grace to the otherwise stocky column.*

6. The Greek Orders
Doric *The earliest and simplest of the classical orders. The fluted columns stand firmly on their platform without intermediate bases. The abacus is deep and plain.*

Ionic *The elegant order is recognizable by the capital of spiral-shaped scrolls called volutes.*

Corinthian *The last and most elaborate order. The tall fluted column was capped by an elaborate stylized carving of acanthus plants. The decorative character of this order made it popular with the Romans.*

6

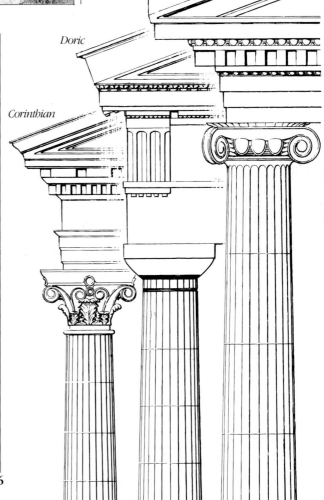

Ionic

Doric

Corinthian

GREEK TEMPLES

1

2

3

4

1. The Acropolis, Athens *(480-430 BC). This limestone hill outside Athens became the site for the most extraordinary collection of temples. They were rebuilt, after destruction by the Persians, by Phidias, the Greek sculptor, in collaboration with the leading architects of the time.*

2. Temple of Poseidon, Paestum, Italy *(450 BC). This Doric building is one of the best preserved of all Greek temples. As the local stone was a coarse and pock-marked travertine, the surface was covered with stucco (or plaster) so the final appearance looked as smooth as Athenian marble.*

3. The Parthenon, Athens *(447-432 BC). This temple of Athena, the largest building on the site, is built entirely in the Doric style. Its sanctuary (naos) contained a gold and ivory statue of Athena. This building is thought to represent the highest achievement of Greek architecture. The combination of sculpture and architecture, stone technology and geometry has never been equalled.*

4. Temple of Nike Apteros, Athens *(427 BC). This tiny Ionic temple has a decorated portico.*

5. Tholos, Delphi, Greece
(390 BC). Doric in style, with Corinthian half columns and an interior paved in marble, the Tholos is just one of the monumental buildings at Delphi, the sanctuary of Apollo, the sun god, and seat of the Oracle.

The Pilgrims' Way at Delphi led a long and calculated route among the buildings, making the most of the natural site to provide new excitements. For a highly symmetrical architecture the informal pathways come as a surprise, a wonderful combination of monumental buildings approached by deceptively casual routes.

5

GREEK SECULAR

1

2

3

1. Theater, Delphi, Greece (c 350 BC). High above the temples, the theater, cleverly contrived from a natural semicircular bowl in the hillside, commands a spectacular view. Like all Greek theaters the use of natural contours made both construction easier and improved the acoustics so that each word sung or spoken on the stage could be clearly heard from every seat. The seating was made out of stone slabs and intermittent aisles of steps provided access.

2. Athenian Treasury, Delphi, Greece (490 BC). An exquisite small building in the lower part of the town. This early Doric structure was the first to be built entirely out of marble.

3. Stoa of Attalus, the Agora, Athens (c 100 BC). A simple but highly public building. In essence it was a simple colonnade, providing shelter against the rain or sun, and linking other public buildings in the Agora. In Athens it provided a place for market stalls, shops and offices. The Stoa of Attalus has been restored by the Americans, one of the most accurate and successful reproductions yet attempted of ancient architecture.

4

5

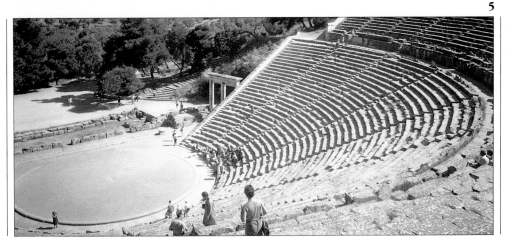

4. Entrance to the Circus, Olympia, Greece *(6th-5th cent BC). This was one of the public areas at Olympia with tiered seating for exhibitions and spectacles. It shows that the Greeks used the arch, albeit for such prosaic purposes as the entrance through which contestants passed into the sports arena.*

5. Theater at Epidauros, Greece *(c 350 BC). With seating for 14,000, this theater has near-perfect acoustics. In the distance can be seen one of the doorways through which the orchestra entered.*

ROMAN EMPIRE

1. The Pantheon, Rome *(AD 120). One of the best preserved buildings in Rome, this was built as a temple to the deities. It consists of a rotunda, roofed over by a dome and illuminated solely by a circular, unglazed opening (26ft/8m) in the crown.*

2. Maison Carée, Nîmes, France *(16 BC). Another well-preserved Roman temple, built in the Corinthian style. Its monumentality is exaggerated by a high, solid base, or podium, which is 12ft (4m) off the ground, and by the single flight of steps on the entrance facade which leads to the deep portico beyond.*

1

2

3

4

5

3. Arch of Constantine, Rome *(AD 312). Triumphal arches were built to celebrate illustrious generals and emperors. The piers between the triple openings record and depict scenes from Constantine's various campaigns against Maxentius.*

4. Hadrian's Villa (reconstruction), Tivoli, Italy *(AD 118-133). The concept of the country villa first started with the Romans who built them to escape city life. Hadrian's villa, as befits an emperor, was a vast complex around a central* *pool. The various structures were based on those seen and admired by the emperor in his travels.*

6

5. Theater, Sabrathah, Libya *(AD 200). A further example of Roman provincial architecture. An immense theater, the seating was semicircular, like the Greeks, but incorporated a huge covered stage where elaborate sets were constructed.*

7. Tomb of the Julii, Saint Remy, France *(25 BC). A three-tiered monument consisting of a decorated base supporting an arched center section which in turn supports a delicate circular colonnade of Corinthian columns. The whole is capped with a cone-shaped roof. Roman tombs were more frequent and elaborate than those of Greece and had more in common with earlier Etruscan models. The Romans practiced both burial and cremation so these tombs contained either the body in a sarcophagus or ashes in an urn.*

6. Rock-cut temple, Petra, Jordan *(c AD 120). Over 700 Roman temple tombs are cut out of the pink rock face of Petra, a trading outpost of Arabia. The free treatment of the architecture shows the unrestrained interpretation of classical form.*

7

ROMAN SECULAR

1

2

3

1. Pont du Gard, Nîmes, France *(c AD 14). Part of an aqueduct system, 25 miles (40km) long, that brought water into Nîmes from the neighboring hills. The bridge is constructed in three tiers of stone arches, the lower two are laid without mortar, and stand some 180ft (55m) above the River Gard.*

2. General view of the market place, Lepcis Magna, Libya *(10 BC). The Romans furnished their colonial possessions with art and architecture as well as the whole structure of their judicial and administrative organization. This market has two circular halls.*

3. Amphitheater, Verona, Italy *(AD 100). Amphitheaters were a Roman innovation, introduced to stage popular spectacles, many of them bloody contests between gladiators, or between men and animals. Oval or elliptical in plan, they consisted of stepped seating in the Greek manner, with arched openings for the entry of processions and combatants.*

4. Insulae, Ostia, Italy *(c AD 50). Tenement buildings, constructed of brick and tile, could be several stories high. The first floor was given over to shops and public rooms, with a vaulted roof of brick and concrete and staircases leading to the apartments. Ostia was an important city and the principal port for Rome.*

4

5

6

5. The Great Bath (reconstruction), Bath, England *(c AD 50). Natural hot water is taken to the pool in lead conduits. A simple Tuscan colonnade still survives around the pool, though the frescoes, which would have decorated the walls, have disappeared. For the pleasure-loving Romans,* baths (thermae) *were an essential part of daily life and were open to all citizens. They were public places for social gatherings and gossip and varied in size from the huge baths of Caracalla (AD 215), which accommodated 1600, down to this more modest one at Bath.*

6. Colosseum, Rome *(AD 70-80). The most magnificent of all Roman amphitheaters and the first to be built entirely above ground, instead of making use of natural contours or terraced hillsides. It is elliptical in plan with seating for 50,000 spectators, and constructed of a series of radiating wedge-shaped buttresses. These were pierced at intervals to permit* lateral corridors, which support sloping concrete vaults, and these in turn carry the tiers of seating. An elaborate network of internal access routes and staircases leads out onto the terraces. In the lowest chambers, at ground level, were caged the wild animals used in combat The curved outer wall has four arched tiers, originally faced in marble.

23

CHAPTER TWO
THE MIDDLE AGES

FROM BYZANTINE TO GOTHIC

INTRODUCTION

The Roman Empire took a long time to die, weakened as much by its own excesses as by incursions and skirmishes with invaders from the north. The seat of Roman power consequently shifted according to circumstances. Emperor Constantine (ruled AD 306-337) was converted to Christianity in AD 313 and the following year moved his capital from Rome to Byzantium, later Constantinople and now Istanbul. The rise of Christianity was to be crucial to the development of Western architecture over the following thousand years.

This millennium is divided architecturally into four periods: Early Christian, Byzantine, Romanesque and Gothic. In each age the Church dominated architecture and the arts, becoming the sole repository of learning throughout what have come to be known, a little unfairly, as the "Dark Ages." Secular buildings were also erected – castles, forts and domestic buildings of all kinds – but they have not endured, nor were they generally as significant as the churches, monasteries and cathedrals.

The poverty and humility of the early Christians was reflected in their buildings. To a people who believed that the Second Coming was imminent, it is not surprising that they were not much interested in building lasting monuments. Instead they preferred to modify or rebuild those Roman buildings which best served their purpose. The chief of these was the basilica, used for administrative purposes in Roman times. The seed of Christianity had been imported by Peter and Paul to Rome and it was from here that the new faith and its buildings were disseminated. Where possible the old buildings were adapted and where new ones were erected, the same style prevailed. This was essentially a simple rectangle on plan, with a semicircular apse at the far end. The rectangle was divided into a central nave with side aisles separated by columns, a general arrangement which was to persist into Gothic times. The nave above the columns was taken up as a plain wall into which windows were pierced to allow light to fall onto the congregation. The apse was roofed by a half dome which later came to be decorated with mosaics.

Byzantine Influence

The first radical change in Christian architecture came with the move to Byzantium, where a stylistic merger took place between East and West. In Eastern building the dome had long been an important feature. Now it became fused with the Western basilica plan, which expanded to form the Greek cross, that is a cross having four arms of equal width and length. This was not only theologically symbolic but liturgically practical.

The cross form came to be roofed with a dome over the central crossing and one above the nave, apse and each transept as well. If you imagine a circle in a square (a

Stave Church, Oslo, Norway
(13th cent). Scandinavian timber churches built from the 11th century onwards. This church, in a folk museum in Oslo, has the traditional corner posts and upright planks.

dome over an apse, say), the structural problem facing the Byzantines is immediately clear. The circle touches the square at four points only, in the centers of the sides, but this is inadequate for structural support of a dome constructed out of the solid masonry. Some way had to be found of distributing the weight of the dome equally so that it could be transferred to columns or piers and so down to the foundations.

The Greeks achieved this by an ingenious method. Imagine again a square on plan with round arches spanning each of the four sides. If a dome is to sit over the square, there will be four roughly triangular sections left at the corners. The architects built these sections up into small, curved semi-domes called pendentives, which formed a stable horizontal rim in which to build the dome. The visual effect of this is stunning: the spectator looks up between the great arches to the wide ring which is supported by pendentives, as if suspended in space. Above this the dome soars. Spatially these buildings are extraordinary; the simple geometry of square, arch and circle beautifully resolved.

The first great Byzantine buildings were naturally in and around Constantinople, where Santa Sophia is the supreme example. The style, so perfectly adapted to the new ritual, rippled back westwards again across the Mediterranean. The Emperor Justinian (527-565) established centers in Ravenna and Sicily where churches combining the old basilica form with the new Byzantine ones are to be found. Greek architects built Saint Mark's cathedral in Venice, which had become a Byzantine trading outpost. About this time, Byzantium itself began to decline, succumbing at last to the Turks in 1453, whereupon the center of power swung back again to the western Mediterranean.

Development of the Romanesque

For some reason the Italians remained wedded to their own basilica plan which they now elaborated with white and colored marbles so that their churches came to resemble decorated ivory jewel boxes. They also developed a style of surface arcading which they built up, tier upon tier, to cover the entire facade, as at Pisa. The famous leaning tower, or campanile, is simply a hollow column of arcades, architecturally reflecting the walls of the cathedral close by.

This style, known as Romanesque, in which the round-headed arch became prominent, spread from Italy to France and Germany, eventually reaching Britain (where it is generally called Norman) through the invasions of William the Conqueror. Away from Italy the prettiness and refinement fell away. For one thing there was no rich marble to hand and social conditions in the rest of Europe were so precarious that castles were needed to protect the

INTRODUCTION

The Baptistery, Pisa, Italy
(1153-1278). The Baptistery,
Cathedral and Campanile
make up one of the most
splendid building groups in
Europe. The Baptistery was built
last, and like the others is in the
Italian Romanesque style –
arcades can be seen here on the
first floor. Those above were
gothicized a century later. There
are two domes; a cone-shaped
inner one which can be seen
sprouting from the top of the
larger "false dome."

populace from wandering marauders. Indeed, many
churches, and even cathedrals such as Albi, were built as
fortresses and acted as sanctuaries for their congregations
in troubled times.

Nevertheless the use of simple, if sometimes crude,
ornament persisted, as can be seen in the great churches
of Vézelay in France and Durham in England. Their
architects loved bold geometric patterns of all kinds, and
chevrons, zig-zags, dog toothing and stripes decorate their
churches. They also incorporated naturalistic carving
which, while primitive in execution, is often as direct in its
appeal as more sophisticated work in later art.

Structurally, Romanesque is notable for its mass, its
aesthetic is monumental, its structure conservative. The
round arch dominates everything, repeated again and
again, from huge spans across naves to decorative
arcading high up in the triforium (gallery). Roofs were
barrel-vaulted or simply cross-vaulted with structural ribs.
Nearby older buildings were often ransacked for materials; marbles from ancient Rome were fitted haphazardly
into the facades at Pisa and Roman tiles into the masonry of
St Albans Abbey.

The Impact of Gothic

The last, and perhaps greatest spontaneous expression of
Christendom, which followed the Romanesque, came to
be called Gothic by condescending later scholars. It was
then a term of contempt for what was considered a
primitive style. The dividing line between Romanesque
and Gothic lies simply in the shape of the arch, not in
itself, it might seem, sufficient distinction. The implication
of this simple development is, however, crucial to the
architecture which followed. Whether the new form
developed from the similar but more rounded Saracenic
arch, or from interlocking arcades of round arches, is
unimportant; what it did for architecture was to liberate
the plan shape of the vault.

A square plan can be roofed, as we have seen, by a
dome or by simple Romanesque cross vaults. But if a
rectangular plan is to be vaulted, then problems arise with
round-headed arches because their crowns will be at
different heights with different spans. Roofing becomes
possible, however, with pointed arches. The radius of the
arches will be different but the general pointed
appearance can be kept constant. This immediately gave
architecture a new flexibility, both in plan and in the urge
to build ever higher and higher, both to the glory of God
and the satisfaction of the populace.

The new style, probably first used at St Denis church
near Paris by the Abbot Suger in 1140, quickly spread over
all Europe. The mixture of an increasing, if still
vulnerable, social stability, together with a rich and
all-powerful church gave rise to the amazing richness of

European art up to the fifteenth century.

Churches no longer had to be fortified. The new technology in stone, achieved largely by trial and error, meant buildings now reached astonishing heights. By means of transferring the outward thrust of the new roof vaults to flying buttresses, which were outside the building, walls could be virtually hung with glass. Churches, like Ste Chappelle in Paris and Chartres Cathedral, became like glass houses where Bible stories, warnings of damnation or veneration of local saints could be depicted in glass cartoons,for an enthusiastic, if largely illiterate, population.

The fervor and excitement of Gothic architecture needs to be experienced in the buildings themselves. Even so, their increasing survival as museums today dilutes the impact they must have had in the Middle Ages.

The early Christian enthusiasm spread. The Crusades were inaugurated to win back the Holy Land for Christendom. Military monastic orders were established for this quest, whose knights protected pilgrims on their way to and from Palestine. These crusaders built their castles and hospices across the Middle East. If the knights survived, they returned to their towns and villages to be commemorated in monuments in the parish churches.

The Gothic age waned as the power of the church started to fail. Learning no longer became the sole prerogative of the monastery; people's status in the universe was re-examined. The old, long forgotten classical learning began to excite intellectuals, interest in science stirred. The church fought a rearguard struggle but its grip was loosening.

The revolution which followed was the Renaissance, or rebirth, an age in which art and science, justice and philosophy, literature and economics all combined, for a few brief centuries, to flower together and bring into the world a most extraordinary cultural explosion.

Hardwick Hall, Derbyshire, England (1597). Smythson. The predominant feature of this Elizabethan mansion is the large number of windows. The two towers are topped by decorative stonework incorporating the letters ES after the owner, the Duchess of Shrewsbury.

BYZANTINE & RUSSIAN

1

2

3. Cathedral of St Basil the Blessed, Moscow, USSR (1555-c 1650). A colorful, eight-domed cathedral, situated at one end of Red Square. All the domes have different decorations. The plan is in an eight-pointed star.

1. St Michael the Archangel, Moscow, USSR (1505-9). The facade shows the influence of Italian architects working in Russia at the turn of the sixteenth century.

2. Santa Sophia, Istanbul, Turkey (532-37) Now a mosque, this superb example of the Byzantine style is a square on plan with giant piers supporting the shallow central dome.

4

4. San Vitale, Ravenna, Italy *(AD 32-47). This early Christian church consists of two octagons, the inner one supporting a shallow dome made of clay pots covered by a timber roof. The interior is richly decorated with mosaics.*

5. Little Metropolis, Athens *(1250). This tiny cathedral (38 × 25ft/11.5 × 7.5m inside) is faced with marble taken from ancient Greek buildings.*

6

5

7

6/7. San Foscara, Torcello, Venice, Italy *(1008). This early church is built on a shallow island in the Venetian lagoon. The marble columns, deriving from the Corinthian, with their simple round arch arcading, are typical of early Byzantine church architecture. They are restrained by iron crossbars.*

BASILICAS & MOSAICS

1

2

1/2. San Apollinare in Classe, Ravenna, Italy *(534). A typical basilica church, deriving from Roman secular architecture. This building is a beautiful example of Ravenna's great period under Justinian (6th cent). The exterior is of simple brick with tiled roofs, and the composition is set off against a round campanile, or bell tower. The interior walls and arcades are decorated with mosaics of great originality and spirit.*

The mosaics are different from other Byzantine work in their use of fresh greens, blues and white. This suits the light and unpretentious buildings they decorate and is in contrast to the golds, reds and blacks of Balkan churches.

3

3. San Apollinare Nuovo, Ravenna, Italy *(490). The intricate nave arcading supports a plain wall decorated with mosaic saints. High windows, called clerestories, throw light down into the nave. The roof is simple and flat. At the altar end is a half-round apse roofed by a half dome.*

4. Dome of the Katholikon, Monastery of Hosios Lukas, Greece (c 1020). The dome and its pendentives are covered with gold and colored mosaic. The engineering contribution of Byzantine architecture was in resolving the problem of how to place a circular dome over a square plan – the bottom ring of the dome rests on partly domed corner sections called pendentives which in turn transferred the weight to adjacent walls and piers.

5

5. Church, Daphni, Greece (c 1080). Greek churches developed their individual Byzantine style. The huge mosaic Christ at Daphni appears as if looking down from heaven through the golden dome.

ROMANESQUE

3. Notre Dame du Port, Clermond-Ferrand, France *(12th cent). View from the nave looking towards the sanctuary shows the characteristic treatment of the round-headed arches forming the eastern apse.*

1. St Gilles Priory Church, Gard, France *(1140). The facade of this church shows the change from the simplicity of earlier religious buildings. The doors at the west front are decorated with Romanesque sculptures.*

1

3

4

2. Lucca Cathedral, Italy *(1150). In Italy, Romanesque churches kept to the early basilica plan and construction but became more decorated as the arcading shows here on the marble facade.*

2

4. Ste Madeleine, Vézelay, France *(1089). This massive church in Burgundy illustrates the fortress-like construction of early Romanesque buildings. The round arches are decorated in a striking but primitive manner.*

5

6

5/6. St Mary Church, Iffley, Oxford, England (1175). This little church has much in common with contemporary churches in Normandy. The structure is simple and the repeated use of the Roman arch and arcade provides the architectural character of the facade. The supporting columns of the doorway share Byzantine-like capitals incised with figures and beasts. The outer arches have characteristic zig-zag decorations, while the inner entrance arch is richly sculptured with heads and stylized flowers.

7

7. Durham Cathedral, England (1110-30). The pillars in the nave bay in this, the finest Romanesque cathedral in Britain, are decorated with chevrons and intricate surface patterns (diapers). The cathedral is sited above the river banks of the city.

MEDIEVAL CITIES

1

3

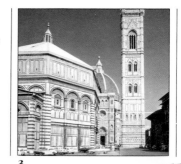

2

4

3. Baptistry & Giotto's Tower, Florence, Italy *(1290 & 1334). The Baptistry was a Romanesque structure but altered in 1290 when the decorative marble was applied in stripes, panels and blank arcading. The free-standing campanile, known by its designer's name, is a Gothic building replacing an earlier tower. These two buildings, together with the cathedral, form one of the greatest groups of religious buildings in Europe.*

1. San Miniato, Florence, Italy *(1013). A beautiful Italian basilica church showing the early use of paneling in green and white marble. This facade is unquestionably classical, but neither truly Roman nor later Renaissance. The elements have been assembled naively but with delightful effect.*

2. *The interior of San Miniato shows the Roman basilica construction. The green and white marble paneling has been carried through above the arches; a form of decoration which remained popular in Italy to Renaissance times.*

4. Santa Maria del Fiore, Florence, Italy (1296). Designed by Arnolfo di Cambio in a Gothic style which was wholly Italian and looks forward in general composition to the Renaissance. After di Cambio's death Giotto took over, followed by other architects.

The roofing of the huge crossing was not started until 1420 when, as a result of great technical difficulties, the work was put to competition. The successful competitor was the early Renaissance designer and architect, Brunelleschi.

5

6

5/6. St Mark's Cathedral, Venice, Italy (1063-85). This great Byzantine building was built by Greek refugees. The basic plan of the Greek cross can be seen, with domes above the nave, crossing and apse, and one over each transept. Later, the upper tiers of arches were transformed by sculpture and decorations of all kinds. The interior view of St Mark's shows how the walls, domes and arches are covered in mosaic. The original figures can be seen in the background – the large one to the right is a later addition which conflicts with the aesthetic and scale of the original.

MEDIEVAL STRUCTURES

1

2

3

4

1. S Maria della Spina, Pisa, Italy *(1323). A miniature church built on the edge of the River Arno. It expresses the Italian Gothic style to perfection.*

2. King's College Chapel, Cambridge, England *(1446-1515). This Perpendicular chapel is one of the rare Gothic buildings which might be described as both Classical and Modern: Classical in its unity and balance, and Modern in its open expression of structure. Unlike many larger churches of the time, it benefited from consistency of style and a simple rectangular plan.*

3. Lavenham Church, Suffolk, England *(c 1500). Lavenham in the early sixteenth century was a rich center for the wool trade and this church reflects its prosperity. The Gothic architecture is by now quite sophisticated: the nave windows and upper clerestories are carefully related, large and almost square, presaging later secular buildings.*

4. Westminster Abbey, London *(1250). The most French of English churches. This view from the cloisters shows the system of flying buttresses that take the thrust of the nave vaults to the vertical piers, which in turn distribute the load down to the foundations.*

5. Milan Cathedral, Italy *(1385-1485). The last great flowering of European Gothic. Milan was actually completed after the first Renaissance buildings had been built in Florence. Considered "debased" Gothic by some, few visitors fail to respond to its huge, airy interior or to the glory of this west facade.*

5

CATHEDRALS

1

2

1/2. Monreale Cathedral, Sicily (1174). This building combines qualities of the Roman basilica with Byzantine-like capitals and mosaics. The Saracenic-pointed arch adds a Gothic dimension. The arch is slightly rounder than true Gothic, though some authorities believe this shape traveled northwards through France to form the familiar pointed arch of northern Europe. The interior has fine mosaics.

4

3

3. Salisbury Cathedral, England (1220-60). A classic English cathedral, both in detail and setting. The west front, though decorated, compared with the French is flat, almost unassuming. French cathedrals of the time were generally placed in the center of towns and presented a rich and powerful west front with deeply recessed doorways encrusted with sculpture and decoration. Monastic features at Salisbury include decorated cloisters. The eight-sided building is topped by the tallest spire in England (406ft-123m).

4. Notre Dame, Paris (1163-1250) View of the south transept. The facades were elaborated in imitation of the first Gothic church, St Denis. Notre Dame is the last of these early Gothic churches to have galleries above the aisles. The style of the facade was copied throughout France.

5. Chartres Cathedral, France (1194-1260). Earliest example of High Gothic. The entrance, which confronts a small square, is simple by French standards. The cathedral's great glories are its sculptured figures and stained glass windows (page 42). The quality of their design is unequalled. Nine towers were planned, only two completed: the fine north spire was built in 1506, with no attempt to match the earlier tower to the south (12th cent).

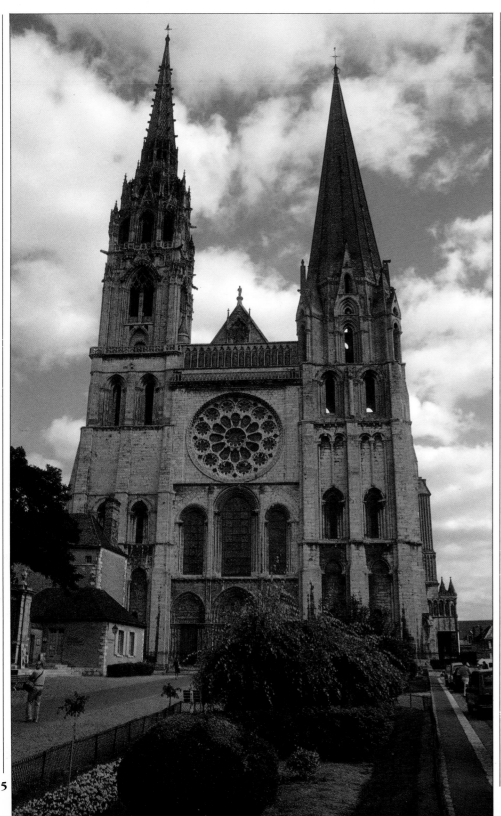

6. Beauvais Cathedral, France (1247-1568). The most extraordinary and daring of all French cathedrals, it stretched stone technology beyond its limits. There were major collapses in 1284 and in 1573. As a result the nave was never finished: all that remains are the choir and transepts. It is the tallest Gothic building, 157ft (48m) to the vault.

7. Wells Cathedral, England (1180-1425). A fine, richly decorated early English nave, terminating with the curious scissor-like bracing at the crossing. The Early English west front is richly arcaded. Its impact derives from its setting among lawns a little way from the town center.

6

7

8. Cologne Cathedral, Germany (1248). The largest Gothic cathedral in northern Europe. The porch detail shows the way Gothic sculptors related their work to the architecture, refining the cruder decoration of Norman carving into controlled cascades of saints and apostles around principal doorways.

8

5

TIMBER FRAME

1

2

1. San Zanipolo, Venice, Italy (c 1300). Early Italian Gothic church with a wooden interior.

2. Henry VII's Chapel, Westminster Abbey, London (1503-19). Fan vaulting reached its most sophisticated form at King's College, Cambridge (page 36), and in this chapel at Westminster. The apparent simplicity of the underlying form is deceptive. Hidden arches above the vaults support the pendants which otherwise seem to defy gravity.

3

3. Chantry Chapel, Wells Cathedral, England (1429). Detail showing an angel bearing an armorial shield. Chantry chapels were endowed with money for the saying of masses for the souls of those who built them.

4. Trunch Church, Norfolk, England (c 1500). Fine Perpendicular ceiling in this parish church displays the ingenuity and craftsmanship with which East Anglian carpenters sought to elaborate their roof trusses.

4

5

6

5. Little Moreton Hall, Cheshire, England *(1550-59). Detail of the black and white patterned walls of this half-timbered, moated house. The bays are hexagonally shaped and a projecting gallery was added in 1580.*

6. Barn interior, West Amesbury, Wiltshire, England. *Up until the seventeenth century when good timber became more expensive and scarce, barns were often cruck framed with large curved timbers meeting at the pointed arch.*

STAINED GLASS & CASTLES

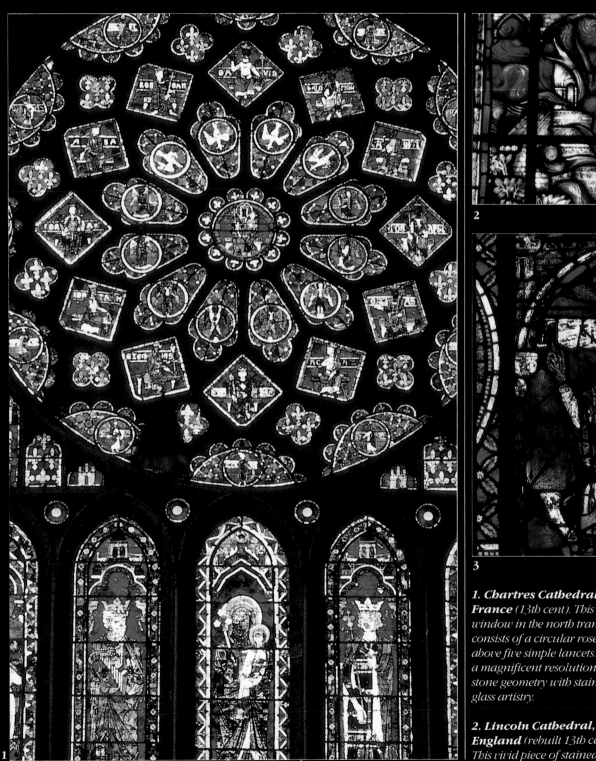

1

2

3

1. Chartres Cathedral, France (13th cent). This huge window in the north transept consists of a circular rose above five simple lancets. It is a magnificent resolution of stone geometry with stained glass artistry.

2. Lincoln Cathedral, England (rebuilt 13th cent). This vivid piece of stained glass records the great fire at Lincoln in 1147.

3. Canterbury Cathedral, England (13th cent). The deep blues and reds of this window, commemorating the martyrdom of Thomas à Becket, show clear influences from across the Channel.

4. Albi Cathedral, France
(1282-1390). View from the north. The fortress church shows a Catalan influence, distinct from that of Gothic churches elsewhere in France. The windows are placed high up and solid brick walls are covered with buttresses and pinnacles. The bell tower is an inner keep (donjon).

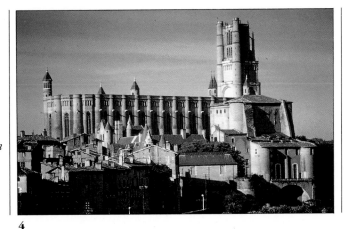

4

5. Krak des Chevaliers, Syria (1252). One of the most astonishing passions of European Gothic was demonstrated in the Crusades, an enthusiasm which went hand in hand with pilgrimages of every kind. Among the many monastic orders were founded military ones whose duty was to recapture the Holy Land from the invading Saracens for Christendom. The Knights of St John were such an order and examples of their building survive across the Middle East, not only churches and monasteries, but also hostels to accommodate pilgrims on their way to and from Palestine. The Knights also built fortifications such as this colossal citadel, surrounded by high walls reinforced at intervals with round towers.

5

6

7

6. The Tower of London
(1078-90). Started under William I but building continued over many years. The Norman foundation can be seen in the chapel and keep. The four-story keep, with its corner turrets, is built in the center, surrounded by concentric, fortified walls, and a moat, long since drained.

7. Caernarvon Castle, Wales (c 1285). Built by Edward I in an attempt to subdue the unruly Celts. Caernarvon follows the classic castle pattern of high-battlemented walls and towers surrounding a keep and quarters for those who lived under its protection.

CHAPTER THREE
THE RENAISSANCE

FLOWERING OF ARCHITECTURAL TALENT

INTRODUCTION

Even after the obvious and logical explanations for the Renaissance have been examined and argued the results remain obstinately miraculous. The very term "Renaissance Man" implies a figure now lost for ever. Shakespeare would deserve the title, yet it could be argued that he merely confined himself to writing plays and occasional verse. In and around Florence, in the mid-fifteenth century, there appear to have been so many all-rounders that it is hard to comprehend how so much versatility in different fields could have been contained in single individuals. To take a few examples: Filippo Brunelleschi (1377-1446), designer of the first Renaissance building, the Foundling Hospital in Florence, was by training a goldsmith, then sculptor, architect and engineer – equally accomplished at these arts. Leon Battista Alberti (1402-72), known to us principally as an architect and theorist, was also an athlete, playwright and musician. The genius of Leonardo da Vinci (1452-1519) hardly needs further elaboration. Michelangelo (1475-1564) was an outstanding painter and perhaps the greatest sculptor of all time, but he was, besides, a military engineer and architect of exceptional brilliance. He also wrote sonnets. What combination of historical events or genetic accident led to this great flowering of talent, invention and intellectual curiosity?

With hindsight it is easy to provide facile explanations. Gothic was played out as a style, the overriding supremacy of the Church was weakening and with the rise of trade and general prosperity there was more leisure for study and retrospection. Also, the greatest manifestations of Gothic had not been in Italy, where Romanesque and Byzantine influences still lingered, but in Northern Europe. The final triumph of the style in Italy had been Milan Cathedral, considered by some to be decadent but by others as an extraordinary and unique building on its own, poised between medieval and a new but non-classical style. The same might be said, a century later, for the Perpendicular of King's College Chapel. It is tempting to speculate whether, in the absence or postponement of the Renaissance, a new architecture altogether might not have developed from Milan. As it happened such guessing is fruitless because, before the cathedral had even been finished, the first Neo-Classical buildings, based on studies of the Roman Antique, were already standing a few hundred miles to the south.

This was also the age of Humanism, a term which has no connection with its modern meaning as the cult of Man in the absence of, or opposed to, God. Rather it meant the opposite, the expression of God through man, in whose image God had been revealed. Nevertheless, it did give man more status than before, and his place in society and under civic law became as important as his relations with the Church. The rise of trade and banking launched the

Arsenale Portal, Venice, Italy (1457). The appearance of the Renaissance in Venice. This bridge was modeled on a Roman arch from antiquity.

great families like the Pitti and the Medici, resulting in a devolution of power and patronage into secular hands. Libraries were assembled or re-assembled, universities founded and old censorships relaxed. Society became more stable, though the times were still turbulent. Italy was still a country of autonomous city states, constantly at odds with one another. Yet in spite of the uncertainties of daily life, the new movement seems to have thrived positively on conflict and feuds.

Neo-Classicism

Architecturally the Renaissance was nourished on Vitruvius (1st cent BC), an early Roman historian whose neglected manuscripts (*De Architectura*) had recently come to light. It was as if a torch had been taken to tinder: painters, architects and sculptors rummaged among the antique for fresh inspiration to bring to their arts.

The first building in the new classicism is generally accepted as being Brunelleschi's Ospedale degli Innocenti (1419-24). About the same time, he was busy spanning the great octagon of the Gothic Cathedral in Florence with a vast dome, a project won by competition. There followed other buildings. Among them the exquisite little chapel built for the Pazzi family in the cloisters of Santa Croce, Florence, where he adopted both Roman and Byzantine forms to create a building that is wholly Florentine.

The face of Gothic was changed by the new vault and the first modest buildings in Florence were radically to alter the architectural face of Europe and, in due course, the whole world. The Renaissance quickly gathered force and spread unchallenged across Italy.

The Architects

The new architects were scholars, no longer master masons or monks, and the invention of printing spread the new vocabulary more quickly and effectively than by

INTRODUCTION

Villa Madama, Rome
(1517). Raphael (1483-1520). A reconstruction of a Roman villa (never completed). This part of the interior was exquisitely decorated by Guilio Romano and others to Raphael's designs which were based on those in the ancient Roman palaces.

the traveling guildsmen of medieval Europe. The first great treatise, *De Re Aedificatoria* by Alberti, was published in 1485 and remained a standard text book. Alberti had gone back to Greek geometry and rules of proportion, and formulated a set of rules based on the proportions of the human form. In this way buildings could be designed in which no part was less important than another in its relation to the whole.

Alberti was no mere theorist. He built a palace for the Rucellai family in Florence and travelled to carry out works in Mantua and Rimini. Rome was next to succumb. Donato Bramante (1444-1514), a Florentine by birth, went to study there and stayed for the remainder of his life. He was responsible for a small but extremely elegant colonnaded chapel, the Tempietto (1502), which was to have a wider influence in Europe than its size would seem to warrant. On a vaster scale, Bramante prepared the original designs for St Peter's, but on the death of Pope Julius II, he was dismissed and his plans were superseded by other and lesser architects. Bramante died in 1514, and by this time the Renaissance was well established. The second generation saw a distinct change of mood.

Mannerism

For convenience the Renaissance movement is sometimes divided into Early Renaissance, Mannerism, Baroque and Rococo. The word Mannerism requires an explanation. It has come to describe the reaction to any new style (though strictly speaking it is a Renaissance term), which is deliberately idiosyncratic and often theatrical. Mannerism of a kind can be seen elsewhere, in the late French Gothic for example, and English Decorated. It is also, perhaps, a lazy way of describing an individual talent whose place in architectural history cannot easily be catalogued or slotted into historical sequence. Such a talent was undoubtedly shown by Michelangelo. He came to architecture late in life, as if painting the Sistine Chapel and sculpture had not been enough. His genius as an architect and town planner turned out to be equally great. In the Medici Mausoleum, in which he incorporated his own sculptures of "Night and Day" and "Evening and Dawn," and in the Laurentian Library it is clear that something new and strange was happening, a twist to classicism which was individual, even wayward, and was to lead others towards the Baroque. When he was over 70, Michelangelo completed designs for the great dome over Bramante's crossing in St Peter's, his last major work.

Andrea Palladio (1508-80)

With the death of Michelangelo the first great phase of the Renaissance was over. The initial period of any new movement always seems, viewed with hindsight, to bear a particular freshness and innocence, which later

Loggetta, Venice, Italy (1537-40). Jacopo Sansovino (1486-1570). A meeting place for the nobility. Sansovino was a sculptor and he has achieved a successful integration of sculpted forms into this building which stands at the base of the campanile and opposite the Doge's palace.

generations can never quite recapture. But before we examine the next phase, Baroque, another figure, born 34 years after Michelangelo, must be considered. Andrea Palladio was an architect who pursued and developed a personal vision, dedicated to proportion, which was to influence the whole of European architecture and in particular the buildings of England and Scotland in the eighteenth century.

Palladio was born in Padua, son of a miller. At 13 he became apprenticed as a stone mason and moved to Vicenza where he worked as an architectural sculptor. When he was about 30 he was taken under the wing of an intellectual patron called Trissino, who encouraged him to study the antique in Rome. Returning to Vicenza, Palladio built many villas, public buildings and churches. It is, however, the villa and the refinement he brought to its development that so influenced later architects. These houses were designed, not for the great princes or wealthy and powerful, but for a new category of the upper classes, increasingly educated and literate, who wanted houses which were both convenient and sensitively designed. The astounding variety of Palladio's villa designs and their tireless search for architectural perfection make him a radical, attractive figure in the European classical tradition.

ISLAMIC INFLUENCES

2/3. Court of Lions, The Alhambra, Granada, Spain *(1309-54). The most famous of all Moorish buildings in Spain, the Alhambra was part of the royal palace and pleasure gardens of Caliph Abd-el-Walid. The delicacy of the structure and elaboration of detail is typical of Saracenic architecture.*

The detail of an arched opening gives an idea of the extraordinary abstract decoration of the walls. Moslem architecture reached as far west as Spain and east to India.

1. Alcazar, Seville, Spain *(1350-69). The word Alcazar derives from El Kasr, the castle. The Moors captured Spain in the eighth century and built mosques, often in the form of unroofed courtyards. The multifoil arches and decorated spandrels are clearly Saracen, but the Moors also looted Roman remains for columns and other material and seemed happy to combine local styles with their own.*

4

5

6

4. Cathedral, Cordoba, Spain (785). *Adapted from a mosque in the sixteenth century. The shape of the arches is Saracenic, but the general effect of arcading, with blind interlocking arches, has a Byzantine, even Romanesque air. Cordoba was at that time the center of Western Islam.*

5. Prayer niche, Madrassa, Isfahan, Iran (1580). *A wonderful detail in dazzling blue tiles. The outside arch is simply painted and well proportioned. Of particular interest is the "stalactite vault" which is really a row of stylized pendentives used to support the upper part of the curved niche.*

6. Mosque, Fatehpur-Sikri, India (1568-75). *Part of the abandoned city of King Akbar, showing the magnificent gateway whose simple pointed arch is reflected in profile by the dome on the left. The roofline silhouette of tiny cupolas is typical of Mogul architecture.*

ALBERTI & BRUNELLESCHI

1

4

2

3

5

6

1. S Maria Novella, Florence, Italy *(1458-60). Facade by Alberti. A church built by the Dominicans in 1350 so that its structure is essentially Gothic. In 1460 Alberti provided a Renaissance front in which the old basilica form is resolved, by the additions of two huge scrolls, into a unified facade.*

2. S Andrea, Mantua, Italy *(1470-72). Bernardo Rossellino (1409-64). Another early Renaissance facade by Alberti. This skilful exercise, based on the Roman triumphal arch, provides a monumental entrance to the church.*

3. Palazzo Rucellai, Florence, Italy *(1446-51). Alberti. This formidable exterior marked a new departure in palace architecture. The stone facade is severe, with three stories divided into bays by pilasters – flat columns which protrude only a few inches beyond the wall. The apartments are reached from an internal courtyard, a plan which remains popular in Italy to this day.*

8

4. Ospedale degli Innocenti, Florence, Italy *(1419-44). Brunelleschi. Trained as a goldsmith, Brunelleschi was also a great sculptor and engineer. This simple and elegant hospice is one of the first true Renaissance buildings. The colonnade is of Corinthian columns supporting arcading which is decorated by ceramic plaques by Luca della Robbia.*

5. Pazzi Chapel, Florence, Italy *(1429). Brunelleschi. A tiny church built within the cloisters of Santa Croce. Based on Roman temple prototypes, it is, nevertheless, an entirely Renaissance building and one of the most delightful by this great architect.*

6. Palazzo Pitti, Florence, Italy *(started 1440). Brunelleschi. The rough hewn stones of the facade add to the fortified appearance. Note the curiously Florentine detail of Saracenic-shaped arches above the door and window openings. Behind this, on the garden side, the architecture is notably more relaxed.*

7. The dome of Florence Cathedral, Italy *(1420-34). Brunelleschi. This famous competition design was set to find a solution for covering the Gothic octagon of Florence Cathedral. Brunelleschi solved the problem by constructing double shells supported on stone ribs. A heavy lantern crowns the dome. The red-tiled exterior, soaring above the roofs of Florence, dominates one of the greatest of all city landscapes.*

8. San Lorenzo, Florence, Italy *(1419-25). Brunelleschi. The Romans would have instantly recognized this as a basilica church, where the rows of Corinthian columns are impeccably Classical.*

7

51

ITALIAN PALAZZI

1. Palazzo Rezzonico, Venice, Italy *(started 1667). Longhena. After the Baroque splendors of his Salute, this Venetian palace by Longhena is restrained; Baroque features are limited to the deeply modeled treatment of the facade. A typical Venetian palace, its glory is directed towards the Grand Canal which formed not only the High Street of Venice, but also its great artery of continuous display and pageant.*

2. Villa Farnesina, Rome *(1508). Baldassare Peruzzi (1481-1536). Like so many of his contemporaries, Peruzzi was trained as a painter and collaborated with Raphael to decorate this beautiful and sensitive villa, one of the most refined of all early Renaissance buildings. The square attic windows are ingeniously incorporated in the frieze just below the main cornice, a device copied by Classical architects as late as the nineteenth century.*

2

1

3. Palazzo Vendramini, Venice, Italy *(1481). Pietro Lombardo (c 1435-1515). Facade architecture but with such an accomplished composition few would complain. The front faces the Grand Canal, so the sides and back are quite plain. The lowest floor is straight onto the water: the principal floor, or piano nobile, is on the second floor with a long balcony for seeing events on the Canal and being seen in return. Although Renaissance in detail, the first impression is still distinctly Venetian Gothic.*

3

4

5

6

4. Palazzo Bevilacqua, Verona, Italy *(1527). Michele Sanmicheli (c 1484-1559). The experience Sanmicheli earned as a designer of military fortifications seems reflected in this robust facade with its heavily rusticated lower story and massive iron window grilles. The effect is lively and muscular, qualities which impressed the younger Palladio, who nevertheless refined this Mannerist approach to suit his own more scholarly style.*

5. Palazzo Strozzi, Florence, Italy *(1490-1536). Benedetto da Maiano (1442-97) with Cronaca (1454-1508). An uncompromising palazzo in which the horizontals are ruthlessly expressed, culminating with the huge and deeply overhanging cornice. The heavy texturing of the rusticated facade with its relatively small window openings make it a formidable but magnificent addition to Florentine architecture.*

6. Palazzo Uffizi, Florence, Italy *(1560-74). Giorgio Vasari (1511-74). Vasari is a colorful figure of the Florentine Renaissance. Today he is best known for his racy, if unreliable* Lives of the Painters, *in which his devotion to Michelangelo is eulogistically expressed. Echoes of Michelangelo are also evident in his only major work, the Uffizi, originally built to house art treasures of the Medici and now a public gallery. The simple fenestration of the top story is almost modern looking, reminiscent of industrial building of the early nineteenth century.*

BRAMANTE

1. Santa Maria della Consolazione, Todi, Italy (1508). Cola da Caprarola (dates unknown). This unusual church is based on the old Byzantine Greek cross plan, but unlike San Marco in Venice, for example, it is very tall and tightly integrated. Here is the archetypal Renaissance dome, supported on a high drum, which was to be repeated all over Europe in the following centuries.

1

2. Tempietto in San Pietro in Montorio, Rome *(1502-10). Bramante. The first great Roman architect of the Renaissance was Bramante. This tiny circular chapel is built within the courtyard of an earlier church. Its perfect scale and detailing combine to make this delightful building monumental, in spite of an internal diameter of a mere 15ft (4.5m). This little temple was to influence later architects in buildings many times the size of the original.*

3. Certosa, Pavia, Italy *(1473). A façade added to an earlier Gothic church, though any traces of the original have been adapted or concealed by the new architecture. It is an extraordinary achievement, carried out entirely in different marbles and decorated by the greatest sculptors of the day.*

4. S Biagio, Montepulciano, Italy *(1519-26). Antonio da Sangallo, the elder (1455-1534). Sangallo was apprenticed to Bramante and went on to design the Farnese Palace, on which Michelangelo also worked. This church has an interesting and ingenious design, in which a square bell tower fits snugly into one of the recesses left by the Greek cross plan. To complete the composition, a Bramante-like dome sits high over the crossing. The actual façade is remarkably restrained, giving the pedimented door and window openings greater vitality.*

2

3

4

MICHELANGELO

1

2

3

1. The Capitol, Rome (1546-92). Michelangelo's astonishing talents also included town planning. On a hill overlooking the Forum, he created an irregular piazza with buildings on three sides. The visitor approaches up a long and wide staircase, so that the piazza slowly opens up, step by step, flanked by huge antique statues. The prospect at the top provides one of the most theatrical and extraordinary experiences in Western city landscapes.

2. The opposite angle, from the Palazzo del Senatore, shows the dramatic star-shaped paving, at the center of which Michelangelo placed the ancient Roman bronze statue of Marcus Aurelius.

3. One side of the piazza is taken up by the Capitoline Museum. In this building Michelangelo used the "giant order," that is a column or pilaster taken up the full height of two or more stories. In this example, the Corinthian pilasters add great dignity to the facade.

4

5

6

4. St Peter's, Rome
(Completed 1585-90).
Michelangelo was 71 when he
was asked to take over work on
St Peter's. He reverted to the
original Greek cross (the nave
was later lengthened), and
reinforced the piers at the
crossing to take this noble dome,
the most famous and perhaps
most beautiful in the world.

5. Palazzo Farnese, Rome,
(begun 1534). Antonio
Sangallo, the younger (1485-
1546). Sangallo was responsible
for the lower two floors of this
stupendously grand Roman
palace. Michelangelo added the
top story which, unusually high,
is brilliantly controlled by the
heavy Florentine cornice and
decorated frieze. A simple and
dominating facade, one which
inspired Charles Barry in the
nineteenth century in his design
for the Reform Club in London's
Pall Mall.

6. Laurentian Library,
Florence, Italy *(1525).*
Staircase by Michelangelo,
completed by Vasari (1571).
Michelangelo's design for this
triple staircase is a perfect
example of Mannerist
architecture, and forerunner of
the Baroque. It is a clever
solution but one which is at the
same time disconcerting, as are
the recessed wall columns which
seem to be, but are not quite,
supported on the wall consoles
beneath them. From this
moment the direction of the
Renaissance was subtly altered.

ITALIAN MANNERISM

1

3

1. Palazzo Massimi, Rome
(1535). Peruzzi. A pupil of Bramante's designed this small palace on a difficult curved site on a busy Roman street. The treatment of this facade is faultless: an imposing first floor of columns supporting a heavy cornice, with a floor above (piano nobile) of tall windows linked by blank balconies. The top two stories have simple framed windows set into deeply cut formal stonework. The wide eaves above accentuate the curving shadows cast on the rounded facade.

2. Palazzo Spada, Rome
(1550). Mazzoni. A Roman palace decorated with stucco reliefs. Stucco is a kind of plaster used externally, where it is relatively resistant to the weather. These decorations add a touch of fantasy to what would otherwise be a correct, almost severe, architecture.

2

3. Palazzo Ducale, Mantua, Italy *(1544). Giulio Romano. Very different from Giulio Romano's Palazzo del Te. The courtyard view shows the extraordinary twisted barley-sugar columns of the principal floor. This approach was called Mannerism and arose from the wish to break away from established classical detailing and explore new forms.*

4

4. Palazzo del Te, Mantua, Italy (1525-35). Giulio Romano. This single story palazzo is the masterpiece of Giulio Romano, a pupil of Raphael and himself a gifted painter. The courtyard has linked arches forming a graceful colonnade, broken centrally by a deep, shaded portico with simple pediment. The outside of this building, like the great palaces in Florence, presents a prison-like face to the public. The rough stone base, with arches repeating those above, gives stability to the whole composition.

The garden portico could almost be in a villa from ancient Rome. The courtyard of this palace plan is essentially Roman, and the use of strong color reminiscent of buildings uncovered at Pompeii and elsewhere.

5 The Sala dei Giganti, or Room of the Giants, in the Palazzo del Te, shows the amazing frescoes designed by Giulio Romano. Here the links with ancient Rome are broken. These paintings with their three-dimensional accuracy are wholly Renaissance.

5

FRENCH CHATEAUX

1. Palais de Fontainebleau, France (1528-40). Gilles le Breton (fl c 1530). The great courtyard of the Royal Palace shows the haphazard nature of its architectural composition, an informality unthinkable in Italy. A favorite French feature is the steep roof, itself two stories high and lit by dormers – windows projecting forwards from the slope. Another notable feature is the horseshoe staircase, a double serpentine flight of steps so large it encircles a small courtyard of its own at ground level. Italian palaces closed their faces to the public: those in France did the reverse in a public demonstration of power and authority.

2. François I Wing, Château de Blois, France (1514-30). Work started at Blois in the thirteenth century and continued over the next 400 years. This wing incorporates the famous spiral staircase tower. As at Fontainebleau, the slate roof is steeply pitched, with elaborate dormers. The lower windows are incorporated in a strict paneled treatment, in which the solid bays between openings are decorated with carved stone medallions.

3. Château d'Amboise, France (1434). Built during the 100 Year's War, on a strategic site above the Loire valley. Later the château lost its military importance and was added to in early Renaissance times when it acquired a more domestic aspect, becoming the first royal residence.

2

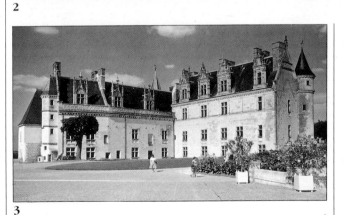

3

4

4. Château de Chenonceaux, France (1557). A later extension of this medieval castle over the River Cher makes Chenonceaux one of the most beautiful of all the Loire châteaux. The picturesque turreted roofline betrays its French authorship.

1

ENGLISH SECULAR

1. Banqueting House, Whitehall, London (1619). *Inigo Jones (1573-1652). After studying the buildings of Palladio in Italy, Jones returned home where he revolutionized English architecture. The severely classical but accomplished banqueting chamber was to have been but a tiny part of a gigantic Palace of Whitehall, which, if it had been completed, would have been among the largest in Europe.*

1

2

3

2. The Queen's House, Greenwich, London (1618 & 1629). *Inigo Jones. The first Palladian villa built in England. The poise and simple authority of this exquisite house literally inaugurated the English Renaissance, providing an example of domestic architecture which has never been surpassed.*

3. Melford Hall, Long Melford, Suffolk, England (1556-59). *Sited near the green in a well-preserved village in rural England, the red-brick Tudor House was built by a sixteenth-century Parliamentarian.*

4

4/5. Broughton Castle, Oxfordshire, England (c 1580). A transitional castle, originally fortified but adapted and extended in quieter times. The general informality is medieval, tempered with the new and only partly understood classical details imported from Europe. The fireplace in the drawing room, Elizabethan in size and importance, is nevertheless Renaissance in its detailing. So is the paneling, with classical decorations applied as if by a pastrycook.

5

6

6. Audley End, Essex, England (1603-1616). The huge mullioned windows, particularly on the second floor, are really Perpendicular in spirit. Classical details are restricted to unambitious mouldings on the first floor.

7

7. Wollaton Hall, Nottinghamshire, England (1580-88). Built by Robert Smythson (c 1536-1614), the castle has a fairytale shape. Its design was revolutionary for the Elizabethan times. The corner towers were placed symmetrically around the masssive central Great Hall.

RENAISSANCE IN EUROPE

1. Palais de Justice, Liège, Belgium *(1526). Because of its geographical position, Belgium was influenced by both French and German neighbors. The French influence here is shown by the roof and semicircular pediment, while the minute clock tower looks Flemish.*

1

2. University of Salamanca, Spain *(1514-29). At first sight this appears to be a Gothic facade, but Renaissance details stand out in the columns and arches, rather as in English Jacobean. This rich period in Spain was marked by a splendid fusion of the two styles before Roman classicism finally took an upper hand.*

2

3

4 5

3. Escorial, Madrid, Spain (1562-84). A distant view of the great, lonely palace and monastery built for Phillip II outside Madrid. The plan is a gigantic rectangle, divided into courtyards with a large central church. The external granite walls are forbiddingly austere.

4. Hôtel de Ville, Antwerp, Belgium (1560-65). Cornelius Floris (1514-75). An early Renaissance building of great distinction and good proportions. The stepped central gable is distinctly Flemish. The top story, which forms an open gallery under the subtly curved roof, is an original and felicitous invention. The building was destroyed in 1576 and immediately rebuilt.

5. Grote Market, Antwerp, Belgium (c 1579). Stepped gables like these were one of the happiest contributions of Dutch and Flemish architecture. The tall windows, huge in proportion to their wall surface, are another characteristic of the period.

PALLADIO

1

2

1. Villa Rotonda (or Capra), Vicenza, Italy
(1550). Palladio. Perhaps the most famous villa in the world, certainly one of the most influential. It was copied widely all over Europe, four times in England alone, and the United States. The direct symmetry of the plan can be seen clearly from the corner view. It is constructed in brick which was plastered; stone was restricted to important mouldings and sculpture.

2. Villa Barbaro, Maser, Italy (c 1560-68). Palladio. A simple but perfectly balanced composition, the antithesis of the Villa Rotonda. The living quarters are provided in the wings, behind the portico at second-floor level. The interior is famous for frescoes by Veronese.

An example of Palladio's temple-like facade (right), the crisp and unusually ornate Corinthian portico has a sculptured pediment.

3

4

3. Palazzo Chiericati, Vicenza, Italy (started 1550). Palladio. The grandest town residence by Palladio. Originally on the outskirts of Vicenza, it is now surrounded by the town. The double loggia facade must have impressed Inigo Jones, for it is clearly the inspiration for the Queen's House at Greenwich. However, the facade is inside-out, with a recessed portico centrally at second-floor level.

4. Villa Badoer, Rovigo, Italy (c 1554). Palladio. All the hallmarks of this great architect are here: a massive flight of steps leading up to an elegant portico, flanked by bare walls pierced with simple openings. Smallest details of proportion and ornament were highly calculated.

5

6

7

5. Teatro Olympico, Vicenza, Italy (1580). *Palladio. This theater has a permanent stage set with a street scene in false perspective, so that in reality it is only a matter of feet in depth. It is based on early Roman models. The sculpture and detailing are magnificent.*

6/7. San Giorgio Maggiore, Venice (c 1556). *Palladio. The simplicity of this cloister is deceptive, and results from a scrupulous attention to solid and void, embellished with meticulous architectural ornament. The cool Palladian interior shows the dome over the crossing supported on plain pendentives. The choirs are screened and set off against white plastered wall and vaults.*

CHAPTER FOUR

THE NATURE OF BAROQUE

CHANGES IN FORM

INTRODUCTION

As the Renaissance was founded in fifteenth-century Florence, so its continuation through Mannerism to Baroque was a Roman inspiration. The term Baroque has come to be attached to architecture (and more recently, to music), but its origins are really much deeper, profoundly associated with religion, painting and literature.

The Counter Reformation in the late sixteenth century made Rome an uncomfortable place in which to live. Powered by the ascetic founder of the Jesuits, St Ignatius Loyola, the movement had introduced the purging of heretics and with this the Inquisition. Visitors from more easy-going republics like Venice found Rome a joyless city. Masquerades and pageants declined, or were forbidden. Michelangelo, himself an ascetic, offered his services to design the new church of the Gesù for nothing. His later works are suffused with feelings of disquiet, ambiguity and barely contained violence. Nudity in painting, except for impeccably religious purposes, gave way to figures clad in draperies which were voluminous and exaggerated, full of restless movement. Three-dimensional representation was heightened by the use of theatrical lighting – "chiaroscuro" (light and dark), the new and dramatic technique in painting characteristic of painters such as Caravaggio and Tintoretto.

The new movement infected architecture. The fluent Mannerism of Guilio Romano (1492-1546) gave way to the expressionism of Bernini and Borromini. Elements of cruelty, sexual repression and violence found outlets in the new art and suited exactly the dramatic evangelism of the Jesuits. Perhaps for this reason the Baroque has always been unpopular in the Protestant north. The great English Victorian art critic, John Ruskin, termed it the "Grotesque Renaissance," recoiling in distaste when he found examples of it shoulder to shoulder with the early churches and palaces of his beloved Venice (page 99). Interestingly enough this lack of sympathy for the style in architecture did not extend to painters like his beloved Tintoretto, a Baroque painter of genius above all others.

The New Forms

Other factors besides religion and painting refueled the new style. The Renaissance discovery of the laws of perspective had led to a revolution in three-dimensional representation. Draperies became both more naturalistic and exaggerated: similarly in achitecture the old forms of square, rectangle, circle and dome were found to be worked out. New forms were sought, and among these the oval became predominant, because while geometrical, it could nevertheless be extended or squeezed at will. On plan it could be crossed or integrated with other ovals, giving rise to exotic serpentine shapes, themselves echoed by oval arches, domes and cupolas above. This spatial and restless architecture became the perfect acoustic envelope for the new music. The great church services and masses of Monteverdi and Vivaldi rang

Compania, Cuzco, Peru (1651). Cuzco was the capital city of the Inca people. The domed towers and central arch provide an unusual facade.

out among its curved walls and domes. Religion regained, for a time, something of the theatrical wonder of the medieval past, to which virtuosity, even if highly artificial, added new dimensions of space and theater to further its ends.

The seventeenth century was also an age of intense scientific discovery and curiosity and the effect this had on the arts and religion was significant. Galileo and Copernicus had shifted the Earth away from its previous position as center of the Universe to a humbler status as just one heavenly body among countless others. The new concept of infinity itself was as exciting and disquieting to the artist as it was to the clergy. In this light, the Baroque should be seen as a second phase to the Renaissance, not as a decline or debasement of a pure original. It was an architecture exploring the mystery of space, of worlds beyond the known world, beyond too, the simple philosophical humanism of the preceding century.

Roman Baroque

The two dominating figures of Roman Baroque are almost exact contemporaries and rivals. Gianlorenzo Bernini (1598-1680) was a brilliant sculptor who turned to architecture. His junior by a year, Francesco Borromini (1599-1667), started as an apprentice sculptor but became an architect. The technical virtuosity of Bernini is extraordinary. Nothing shows this better than his sculpture of "Apollo and Daphne." All is movement and its translation into white marble is consummate. It is as far from the monumental classicism of Michelangelo's statues as the new architecture of Borromini was to that of Bramante or Alberti.

Such pagan triumphs as Apollo and Daphne were

INTRODUCTION

tolerated by the Church but Bernini's religious sculpture was equally theatrical. His most celebrated work in this genre is the amazing "Ecstasy of St Theresa" in a side chapel of S Maria della Vittoria in Rome. The semi-reclining figure of the saint, voluminously draped, is lying with her eyes closed in ecstasy. There is an erotic ambiguity to the pose; the figure of the smiling angel does nothing to relieve the emotionally loaded tableau. The Roman family standing to one side, as if at the theater, implies that the agony was laid on for their entertainment.

Francesco Borromini

Borromini dealt in different forms. A more private and tortured personality than his rival (he was to kill himself after a period of insanity), his art was abstract, concentrated and deeply personal. Later, he might have been called an architectural Expressionist, and certainly nothing like his manipulation of form had been seen before, certainly not in Europe. Indeed some of his forms, like the strange spiral finial to the church of San Ivo (page 73), seem to owe their inspiration to the ancient architecture of Syria or to the then unknown Far East.

After Borromini, Baroque travelled north, first to Piedmont, then across the Alps to Austria, Germany and Central Europe. It also followed the Catholic trail to Spain and Portugal and from there, in due course, to South America. In other countries it withered or was modified, as in France and England. The Château of Vaux Le Vicompte by Le Vau, south of Paris, is Baroque in its great, oval-domed salon, yet it is clearly restrained by an earlier Classicism. Likewise the Baroque architects of England, Christopher Wren (1632-1723), James Gibbs (1682-1754) and Thomas Archer (1668-1743) never approached the organic suppleness or extremism of a Borromini. Only in the monumental and highly sculptural works of John Vanbrugh (1664-1726) and Nicholas Hawksmoor (1661-1736) are some of the uneasy and equivocal qualities of their Italian inspiration manifested. Seaton Delaval by Vanbrugh in Northumberland, and Christchurch, Spitalfields in London by Hawksmoor, both display an unnerving remoteness quite foreign to the gentler Palladianism of their contemporaries.

Rococo

After Borromini, it might seem that nothing further could possibly be accomplished in this direction. Curiously enough the final phase of Baroque, the Rococo, was triggered by interior decoration in France. The term Baroque derived from an Italian word meaning flawed pearl, and Rococo derived from the French *rocaille*, the sea rocks and shells from which a new form of ornament was introduced. It suited the French style and its fantastic forms, free and wholly decorative, came in time to modify and lighten the Baroque superstructure itself. Its greatest genius was shown in the

Ecstasy of St Theresa, S Maria della Vittoria, Rome (1645-52). Bernini. The dramatic presentation embodies the essence of the Baroque and its vital link between sculpture and architecture. Never before had religious subjects been treated with such theatrical and expressionist realism.

churches of southern Germany and Bavaria. In England it was almost entirely an indoor art, carried out in stucco applications to walls and ceilings.

As Baroque had been a reaction to Vitruvian discipline, so it too eventually gave way to a return to earlier Classicism, based on recent archeological discoveries in Greece and Italy. It was never an easy art to master. In the hands of Borromini or Vanbrugh, it is ravishing: in lesser hands it falls too easily into licence and superficial vulgarity. Perhaps of all architectural styles, it is for the toughest and most accomplished talents only.

Claude-Nicolas Ledoux
*(1736-1806). Ledoux's buildings result from a unique interpretation of Italian Classicism. In 1775 he was invited to provide buildings surrounding a saltworks at Chaux in eastern France, a project never fully carried out. The theatrical entrance portico (**1**) places strictly classical columns and entablature against freely carved rocks which symbolize the natural strata of the saline springs themselves, recalling earlier Italian models like the Trevi Fountain.*

*The Director's Stables (**2**) is more like a temple; its rusticated facade and bold geometrical openings elevating it above the merely practical. Likewise, the Director's own house (**3**) is an exercise in the grandiose, yet rescued from pretentiousness by the force of its architectural coherence.*

1

2 3

ROMAN BAROQUE

1 **2**

3 **4**

1/2. Il Gesù, Rome (1568-75). Giacomo Vignola (1507-73). Facade by Giacomo della Porta (c 1537-1602). The classical good manners of the front of the Gesù, with its side scrolls, conceals a more obviously Baroque interior. The style was closely connected with the new Jesuitical movement and this church was designed for the large following which the new order attracted.

Inside, the church shows the early Baroque experiments with space and movement, combined with the richness of the eighteenth-century marble wall coverings. Preaching was an important part of the new form of service and Vignola provided an ample nave and well-lit crossing for the congregation. The church is transitional between Mannerism and High Baroque.

3/4. San Carlo alle Quatro Fontane, Rome (1665). Borromini. A small masterpiece of Roman High Baroque. Squeezed into a tiny site at the corner of a crowded square, this extraordinary serpentine facade conceals an interior of equally sinuous forms and spatial dexterity.

An interior view shows the central, deeply coffered dome, supported on pendentives with oval medallions.

5. S Andrea delle Fratte, Rome *(1653). Borromini was commissioned to complete the interior of this church, the nave of which had already been started.*

5

6. San Ivo della Sapienza, Rome *(1642-60). Borromini. The amazing spiral finial to the lantern which completes the dome of the star-shaped church of the University of Rome. The strange juxtaposition of forms shows Borromini exercising his unrestrained sculptural expressionism.*

6

7. SS Martina e Luca, Rome *(1635-50). Pietro da Cortona (1596-1669). The facade of this church might be described as restrained Baroque. The relationship of the gently bowed central section with the severe corner piers, and the immaculate juxtaposition of the twin storeys displays a mastery of lively composition.*

7

NORTH ITALIAN BAROQUE

1. St Peter's Rome (1506-1626). This famous building was destined to be a monument to Pope Julius II who demolished an earlier basilica church on the site to make way for it. Many architects were involved in its eventful history but Bramante, who provided the original Greek cross plan, Michelangelo, who designed its superb dome, and Bernini, who provided the internal visual impact, were the most important.

2/3. The Colonnade, St Peter's, Rome (1656-67). Bernini. The sculptor-architect Bernini laid out a huge oval piazza in front of the cathedral, flanked by colossal colonnades with double columns each side. The aim, brilliantly realized, was to embrace pilgrims within the two arms of the great mother church, which lay at the focus of the composition.

Inside the cathedral, Bernini provided a huge bronze Baroque baldacchino (1624-33) to stand above the traditional throne of St Peter. The barley-sugar columns are said to derive from the old Temple in Jerusalem, but whatever their origin, their contorted forms appealed to their Baroque designer.

1

2

3

4

4. This view of St Peter's interior shows Bernini's gilt cathedra Petri, topped by a sunburst window. The giant order Corinthian pilasters lend background monumentality.

5. St Maria della Salute, Venice, Italy *(1631-82). Baldassare Longhena (1598-1682). The architect made superb use of one of the great backgrounds of the world, the entrance to the Grand Canal. Here Longhena raised a grand octagonal church with double domes, a three-dimensional mass which presents a rounded composition from every viewpoint. The scrolled buttresses seem to support the main dome.*

5

6

7

6. Basilica di Superga, Turin, Italy *(1715-27). Filippo Juvarra (1678-1736). Juvarra was trained in Rome and brought a freestyle Baroque to his many and versatile projects in Piedmont. His masterpiece here consists of a church and monastery on a hill overlooking Turin. The domed church rises from the end of the long rectangular monastery, in which it is embedded, and is fronted by a high and free-standing portico.*

7. Palazzo Barberini, Rome *(1628-33). This palazzo was designed by Carlo Maderna, another of the architects who worked on St Peter's, but on his death it was completed and given a facade by Bernini. False perspective treatment of the top windows makes their recesses appear deeper.*

FRENCH CLASSICISM

1. Palais du Luxembourg, Paris (1615-24). Salomon de Brosse (1571-1626). Built for Marie de Medici in the Italian style, the formal courtyard plan and steep roof pitches betray an unmistakably French treatment.

2/3. The Louvre, Paris (1546-1878). The south facade. In the sixteenth century François I started work on this palace which was to become one of the largest in Europe. What one monarch erected, another remodeled or rebuilt, with the result that some ten or more architects were involved in its long history. In 1650 Louis Le Vau (1612-70) was commissioned to rebuild half the courtyard of the old palace. With Claude Perrault (1613-88), Le Vau completed the east front in 1667. This consists of a solid base above which double-column giant orders unite the second and third floors.

The internal elevation shows how, on the courtyard side, Le Vau's treatment is less formal, almost domestic in scale. Architectural interest is enhanced by the syncopation of projections and recesses along the facade.

4. Church of Les Invalides, Paris (1679). Jules Hardouin-Mansart (1646-1708). Built by Bruant, the church was completed by Mansart with the famous dome in 1691. Mansart was faced with the perennial problem that from the outside a dome tends to look flatter than it really is, particularly when viewed from below the end of a long nave or transept. To overcome this he built up a series of three domes, one above the other, so that the one seen from outside is in fact "false," constructed of wood and concealing those below, which are viewed from inside.

1

2

3

4

5

6 **7**

5. Place de la Concorde, Paris *(1755). Lay out originally by Gabriel and present form by Hittorf. The magnificent square is flanked by two palaces – Hotel Crillon and Ministère de la Marine. The Place offers perspectives in every direction and was the site of the infamous guillotine during the reign of terror.*

6. Church of the Sorbonne, Paris *(1635-42). Jacques Lemercier (c1585-1654). A city church built for Cardinal Richelieu. A solid first floor of detached columns supports a pedimented second tier of sculptured niches flanked by pilasters. Above this rises an elevated drum, a dome characteristically French.*

7. Panthéon, Paris *(1757-80). Jacques Soufflot (1713-80). A simple Greek cross church entered under a giant order Corinthian portico. This Neo-Classical building bears comparison with St Paul's in London, particularly with Wren's early but rejected model, based on a similar plan. The interior is equally cool and assured, employing modulations of detached columns and pilasters.*

VERSAILLES & ROCOCO

1/2. The Palace of Versailles, France. (1669-1674). Le Vau. Louis XIV's famous palace complex is built around an older hunting palace. The entrance facade is one of the grandest in Europe. The absence of planting and the giant cobbles underfoot add to the brutal approach to this magnificent symbol of France's age of power and influence.

Detail of the gilt ironwork screen to the main courtyard. The finest craftsmen in France were employed to create a standard of luxury and pomp hitherto unknown. This display of extravagance ultimately contributed to the downfall of the monarchy in 1789.

1

2   3

3. The magnificence at Versailles continued into the garden with vast formal layouts by the landscape architect André Le Nôtre (1613-1700). These were based on complex axial avenues which gave the spectator glimpses of lake, fountains and sculptures. The palace on this elevation is, on account of its sheer size, impressive, but the unrelieved roofline makes for monotony.

5

4

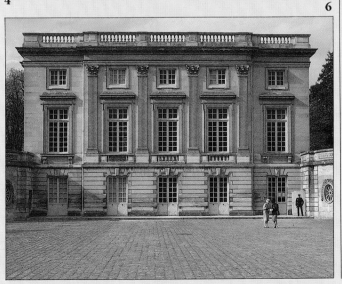

6

4/5. The Chapel at Versailles (1696).
Hardouin-Mansart. France, like England, never entirely succumbed to Roman Baroque, and this example shows that French Classicism retained its sense of order and essentially Renaissance vocabulary.

The interior of the chapel shows Mansart's orginality. Heavy, richly sculptured arches support a much taller colonnaded gallery above, which gives spatial interest and spills broken light into the body of the nave. Baroque splendor, in the form of gilt sculpture, is restricted to the altar and apse.

6. Petit Trianon, Versailles (1761-8). Jacques-Ange Gabriel (1698-1782). By the middle of the eighteenth century there was a return to interest in classical architecture, particularly Greek. This perfect small house was built in the gardens of Versailles by Louis XV and later altered for Marie Antoinette. The excesses of the Baroque are all behind: here is order, proportion and symmetry.

7

7. Vaux-le-Vicomte, Paris (1657). Le Vau. This orderly, lavish château, represents the furthest Le Vau was prepared to take Baroque. A large oval salon is domed over, providing the massive central feature of the garden front. Formal gardens and landscaping by Le Nôtre.

GERMAN BAROQUE

1

3

4

2

1. Upper Belvedere, Vienna, Austria (1720-24). *Lukas von Hildebrandt (1668-1745). Von Hildebrandt was born in Italy and studied with Carlo Fontana in Rome. After further studies in Piedmont, he brought a north Italian Baroque to Austria where he built the huge Belvedere Palace. These dynamic figures support vaults, themselves decorated with trophies, scrolls and light plaster reliefs.*

2. The Zwinger, Dresden, Germany (1711-22). *M. D. Pöppelmann (1622-1736). Built as a kind of large playhouse and pleasure gardens for Augustus of Saxony, it fronts a huge open square in the center of Dresden.*

3/4. Nymphenburg Palace, Munich, Germany (1717-23). *Built in the Bavarian Court style, the outside is formal, almost severe. By contrast, the interior is highly decorated, with flowery plaster relief, gilded or silvered and set against white and colored backgrounds. In imitation of Versailles, four pavilions were added, linked by galleries.*

5

5. Amalienburg Palace, Munich, Germany *(1734). The French appearance of this building in the grounds of the Nymphenburg Palace is no accident as it was designed by François Cuvilliés (1695-1768), a court dwarf who was found to have architectural gifts and was sent to study in Paris. On his return he created, among other works, this charming little summer pavilion. The inside is as light and fluent as the exterior.*

7. Ottobeuren Church, Bavaria, Germany *(1737). Johann Fischer (1692-1766). The design of this Free Abbey church involved a number of architects and an assortment of styles. Fischer modified the plan to emphasize the spatial possibilities. The rococo plaster work, by Feichtmayer, provided the finishing touches of fantasy and architectural illusion. Fischer was responsible for a number of spacious churches whose interiors were ideal for the light, elaborate style of Rococo.*

6

6. Schönbrunn Palace, Vienna, *Austria (1695-1750). Fischer Von Erlach (1656-1723). Designed as a rival to Versailles. The architecture is much lighter, however, and the use of color sets it firmly in Central Europe. Inside, the* decorations are Rococo — fantastic and capricious.

7

81

WREN & CONTEMPORIES

1

2

3. St Mary-Le-Bow, London *(1670-80). Wren's flair and genius is shown by his city churches, particularly in his highly individual treatment of spires. These provided prototypes for later buildings throughout the country and copybook examples for many of the new churches in the American colonies.*

4. Chelsea Royal Hospital, London *(1687). Nothing illustrates the "Wren" style better than this well-mannered hospital for military pensioners. The emerging social humanity of the seventeenth century and its translation into architecture by one of its most civilized practitioners is perfectly demonstrated.*

5. St Stephen Walbrook, London *(1672-77). Wren was an accomplished mathematician and engineer and his skill in both arts is shown in the original and spacious interior of this small city church. Its debt to Baroque is clear, but a debt civilized by the "Age of Reason."*

6. Christchurch, Spitalfields, London *(1723-39). Hawksmoor, for many years an assistant to Wren and Clerk of Works at St Paul's, was a more somber and deliberate architect than his tutor. This church is assembled like some ancient tomb, its tower terminating in an anachronistic but magnificent Gothic steeple. It is one of the most extraordinary buildings of its time.*

1/2. St Paul's Cathedral, London *(1675-1710). Wren. The Great Fire of London (1666) gave Wren the opportunity of redesigning the City; St Paul's was to provide the focal point. Clearly inspired by Italian Baroque, it is nevertheless a restrained and essentially Protestant answer to St Peter's.*

Inside, the spatial qualities of the Baroque are more obvious. The great dome, which is contained by a vast iron chain around its outside perimeter, sits on traditional pendentives going back to the Byzantine.

3

4

5

6

7

7. *Radcliffe Camera, Oxford, England* (1737-49). *Gibbs was unusual among English architects in having studied abroad; he worked in Rome in the studio of Carlo Fontana. Setting up in practice in England, his architecture reflects his attempt to resolve his Mannerist background with contemporary English Palladianism. The circular plan of this domed library perfectly fits its courtyard site; a building of which his tutor would surely have approved.*

ENGLISH BAROQUE

1

2

3

1. Blenheim Palace, Oxfordshire, England *(1705-24). Vanbrugh. Built by the state for the Duke of Marlborough in recognition of his military achievements. Vanbrugh is an attractive figure in English architecture, equally famous as a dramatist. Some of this sense of theater can be seen in his buildings, tempered by the professionalism of his collaborator, Hawksmoor, whose hand can be seen in many of the details.*

2/3. Castle Howard, Yorkshire, England *(1699-1712). Vanbrugh. The greatest of this architect's country houses, the nearest equivalent in English terms to the French château or Italian palazzo. The great entrance lies under the central* *dome and rises the full height of the building, flanked by staircases. Vanbrugh was again assisted by Hawksmoor, but the individual character of the playwright-architect seems to dominate. The severe colonnaded mausoleum in the grounds, however, is wholly Hawksmoor's.*

4

4. Seaton Delaval, Northumberland, England (1718-29). Vanbrugh at his most dramatic and idiosyncratic. This austere Hall sits near the coast, a forbidding and brooding pile, in which Italianate motifs have been welded onto a traditional Elizabethan house plan.

5/6. Royal Naval Hospital, Greenwich, London (1696-1702). Situated on the Thames, one of the grandest architectural prospects in England. Many architects were involved including Wren, Vanbrugh and Hawksmoor, and doubt still lingers on certain attributions. The white building in the far center is the Queen's House by Inigo Jones (page 62), predating the nearer buildings by half a century.

The painted ceiling to the Great Hall at Greenwich was executed in 1707 by Sir James Thornhill who painted the dome at St Paul's. This is perhaps the nearest approach in England to the Baroque splendors of Venice and Rome.

5

6

7

7. Doorcase, Whitehaven, Cumbria, England (c 1700). A fine Renaissance doorway showing the lingering flamboyance of Wren-style detailing. With the approaching Palladianism, such exuberant detailing would be replaced by simpler Classicism.

PALLADIANISM

1

2

4

1. Chiswick House, London (1726). Lord Burlington (1694-1753). The English Palladian villa. With the death of the great Baroque architects, Palladianism became re-established as the predominant English style. William Kent had been sent to Italy to record buildings and on his return collaborated with his patron, Lord Burlington, a talented amateur, on this reconstruction of Palladio's Villa Rotonda (page 66) into a northern and perhaps less appropriate climate.

2. Stourhead, Wiltshire, England (1722). Colen Campbell (1673-1729). If one detaches the later wings, the essentially Palladian villa is re-

vealed. Campbell was one of the most versatile early Georgian architects, devoted to the works of Palladio and Inigo Jones.

3/4. Mereworth Castle, Kent, England (1722-25). Campbell. English Palladianism in the form of an attractive version of the Rotonda (page 66), perfectly suited to its rural park in rolling Kent landscape. There are many plasterwork decorations inside.

3

5

6

5. Holkam Hall, Norfolk, England (1734). William Kent (1685-1748). Another collaboration between Kent and Lord Burlington. All the familiar Palladian details are here, but the size and grouping are essentially English.

6. Horse Guards, London (1742). Kent. Building erected after the architect's death, but to his designs. The native English character is again noticeable: such a military brief would, in Europe, have been more severely treated. The composition would look appropriate in an English park.

ADAM & CONTEMPORARIES

1

1. Osterley Park, Middlesex, England (1761-80). Robert Adam (1728-92).
Adam imposed the new Neo-Classicism onto the bones of an earlier building whose origins are shown by the corner towers. The architect cleverly filled the open courtyard front with a portico based on reconstructions of the Portico of Octavia of Ancient Rome. The visitor passes through this to a courtyard entrance beyond. The interior is meticulously detailed throughout, from ceilings to carpets.

2. Royal Society of Arts, London (1772). Adam
brothers. Between 1768 and 1772, Robert and James Adam built, as their own speculation, a huge terrace called the Adelphi on the Thames, a project which almost brought them to ruin. Today little survives, but this charming building with its characteristic treatment of the central Venetian window still stands in a side street.

3. Syon House, London
(1761). Adam. Many view Adam's greatest achievement as his skill as a decorator. While this may be unfair to his achievements in architecture, there is no doubt that his interiors were both popular and influential. This hall at Syon shows his superb handling of Neo-Classical orders and decorations.

2

3

4. Guildhall, Bath, England
*(1766). Thomas Baldwin
(1750-1820). The influence of
the Adams is unmistakable in
this interior by Baldwin, a Bath
architect who was responsible
for many of the fine streets in this
magnificent Georgian city.*

5. Orangery, Kew, London
*(1761). William Chambers
(1723-96). Orangeries were a
popular form of hot house,
particularly in the colder
climates of northern Europe.
Chambers carried out a
number of works at Kew,
including the famous Pagoda.
In his youth he had studied
architecture in France, and
later hovered between
Palladianism and the Neo-
Classicism of Adam. His most
successful works were his
smaller buildings such as this.
The French influence seems
unmistakable.*

4

5

6

**6. Heveningham Hall,
Suffolk, England** *(1778).
James Wyatt (1747-1813).
Palladian elements contribute
to the lightness of this orangery
in a classical house. It has a* *deceptively nineteenth-century
appearance, a century which
saw the great popularity of that
descendant of the orangery –
the conservatory.*

EUROPEAN NEO-CLASSICISM

1 2

2. La Bourse, Paris *(1807). A.T. Brongniart (1739-1813). Brongniart conceived this stock exchange as a simple rectangle surrounded by a giant Corinthian colonnade, reminiscent of other temple designs of the period – correct if oppressive.*

4. Glyptothek, Munich, Germany *(1816-34). von Klenze. A Greek revival sculpture gallery. This was the earliest of von Klenze's important commissions. The flat pediment, heavily enriched with sculpture like the Parthenon, is typical of the period and bears comparison with the British Museum.*

1. Walhalla, Regensburg, Germany *(1830-42). Leo von Klenze (1784-1864). A monumental work by the German Neo-Classicist. He trained in Paris then returned to Bavaria where he became the court architect. The Greek inspiration is clear; what is novel is the treatment of staircases and parapets which give the building a colossal base as they rise in giant steps above the River Danube.*

3. Altes Museum, Berlin *(1823-30). Karl Friedrich Schinkel (1781-1841). Schinkel was the greatest Neo-Classical architect of Germany, possibly in Europe. He was virtually the creator of modern Berlin, and elements of his style persisted through to the Third Reich and Hitler's favorite architect, Speer. The museum is strictly Classical, but Schinkel was capable of less restrained works, including theater sets for* The Magic Flute.

5. Town Hall, Birmingham, England *(1832). A competition design in a striking temple architecture, one of the purest and most accomplished in the country, where such designs were less popular than in Europe.*

6. Opéra, Paris *(1861-75). Charles Garnier (1825-98). With Garnier, the Greek revival mold of French architecture was broken. If his style can be described, it must be Neo-Baroque, but the Opéra remains an individual and highly entertaining building of immense presence and charm. Garnier was quintessentially French, and a celebration of nationalism runs through his work. The interior is sumptuous.*

3

4

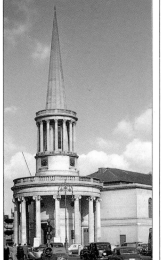

7. All Souls Church, London (1822). John Nash (1752-1835). Nash was the greatest developer/planner of his time and this simple but effective church was sited at the end of his famous Regent Street (since destroyed and remodeled).

GREEK REVIVAL IN THE USA

1. First Baptist Meeting House, Providence, USA *(1774-75). Joseph Brown (1733-85). Unsurprisingly, New England architecture relied heavily on English precedents until other immigrants made their mark with imported styles. The meeting house was a unique architectural structure; it served as a church for the Puritans and was a reaction against the Gothic churches of their homeland. The steeple, clearly modeled on Wren and Gibbs, seems, in a quite proper American way, to be aiming even higher than the originals.*

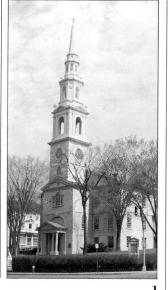

1

2

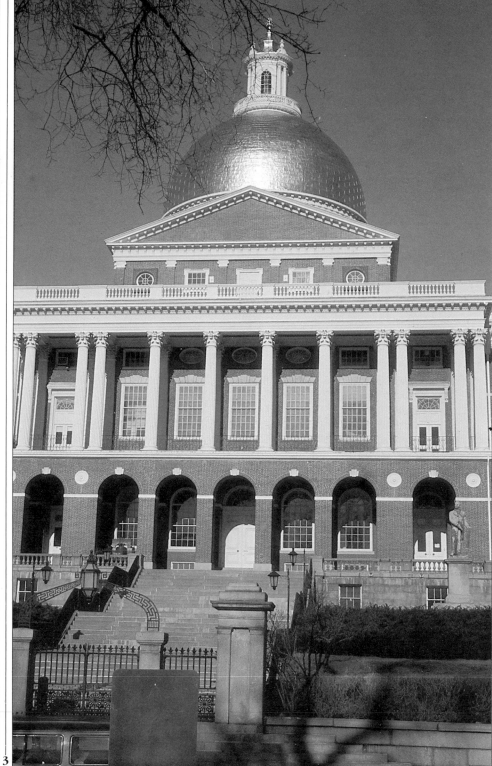

3

2. Capitol, Washington, USA *(1851-63). Thomas Walter (1804-87). Walter worked in many styles before settling down to a respectable and highly competent Neo-Classicism. The famous Capitol dome, on a cast-iron frame, has echoes of St Peter's, Rome, and even more strikingly, the Pantheon in Paris.*

3. Massachussets State House, Boston, USA *(1793). Charles Bulfinch (1763-1844). Bulfinch leaned heavily on British traditions and architecture, introducing an imported Adam style that was individual, yet wholly American. The State House is said to have been inspired by Chamber's Somerset House, but its translation into brick and stone gives it a strong and agreeable colonial flavor.*

4. Monticello, Virginia, USA *(1780-1809). Thomas Jefferson (1743-1826). The third President of the United States was a gifted architect, as can be seen from his own house, Monticello. Jefferson traveled widely and admired a wide range of European buildings. Nevertheless, his own house, while acknowledging an obvious debt to Palladio, is full of highly original arrangements and inventions, products of a man of exceptional talents.*

5. The White House, Washington, USA *(1793-1801, 1829). James Hoban (c 1762-1831). So familiar is this building that it seems a timeless and integral part of axial Washington, even if dwarfed by later competitive monuments on all sides. In fact it is an early neo-Palladian exercise, heavily influenced by Gibbs.*

4

5

6

6. Lincoln Memorial, Washington, USA *(1917). Henry Bacon (1866-1924). One of the last great Neo-Classical monuments of distinction. The date of this Greek Doric temple is surprising: it might have been built in France or Germany a century earlier.*

93

CHAPTER FIVE

THE INDUSTRIAL SOCIETY

NEW TECHNOLOGY

INTRODUCTION

Architecture in Europe before the eighteenth century was still largely an establishment pursuit. Not that a gifted youth like Palladio or Hawksmoor could not rise by sheer talent, but having risen he would find himself taken into an established circle of other professionals and patrons in whose number would be an influential côterie of wealthy, enthusiastic amateurs.

An architect could even get by without distinctive gifts of draftsmanship, providing the information could be put across by other means. In any event, a Clerk of Works or Master Mason would be at hand to translate outline sketches into finished buildings. Nor was any deep knowledge of engineering required. Masters of the art, like Brunelleschi and Wren, were comparatively rare.

These were, in many ways, happy times for architects, without restrictions from any building codes, planning

Bridge, Ironbridge, Shropshire, England (1779-81). Abraham Darby III (1750-91). Now a pedestrian bridge, this 196ft (59m) semicircular bridge was the first iron bridge in the world. It spans the Severn Gorge and was built with iron smelted at nearby Coalbrookdale, the virtual birthplace of the Industrial Revolution.

requirements or the plethora of services now considered essential to modern structures. At that time, too, everyday buildings like smaller houses, farms and shops were put up by builders who relied on architect's copy books for the finer details and general proportions.

The Industrial Revolution

This was not to last. Towards the end of the eighteenth century, changes were abroad which were to be far reaching. They stirred first in England where colonial prosperity, scientific curiosity and cheap coal and iron combined together to bring about what has come to be called the Industrial Revolution. This was to change the face, not just of England, but ultimately the world.

The invention of the steam engine and development of the locomotive led to an immediate revolution in transport.

INTRODUCTION

Coal for furnaces led to improvements in metal manufacture, notably cast iron, which in turn was brought into use for the bridges required for roads and railways. Canal technology flourished. Roads were improved and travel no longer became the prerogative of the rich. The less well-off could move about and did so, deserting a densely populated countryside to look for better wages in the new towns.

With these changes, a new type of designer emerged, more of an engineer/builder than architect. They were tough-minded practical men like Thomas Telford (1757-1834), Joseph Paxton (1801-65) and Isambard Kingdom Brunel (1806-59). Others like Decimus Burton (1800-81), son of a builder, used their practical skills in cast iron to good effect, but in general, architects sought to conceal the new technology under masonry and stucco, or disguise it with ornament. The engineers had no such qualms. Telford's Buildwas iron bridge, Brunel's Clifton suspension bridge and Paxton's great glass houses (culminating in the Crystal Palace) openly celebrated the new material.

Some architects and critics looked on in dismay, perceiving – not so foolishly as it turned out – the threat to the landscape and towns which the new industrialization was bringing in its wake. But the impetus of industry could not be stopped. Its technology spread abroad, finding ready talents to exploit it in France and Italy. It moved to the United States where it took immediate root and provided the foundations for the skyscraper. This was in the future; in the meantime the Classical tradition was slowly waning, and much of the original Renaissance spirit was by now exhausted. Detailing became coarse, infected by the nouveau riche ostentation of the rising middle classes and the fruits of capitalism.

Neo-Classicism

Those who could find no comfort in either an outworn Classicism, or in the more robust works of the new engineers, turned back to the past for comfort and inspiration. Architects were not alone in this flight from reality. The whole of the Romantic movement in literature, painting and music echoes this uncertainty, nostalgia and tension. Walter Scott set his novels in a past at once more colorful and secure. Literary medievalism coincided with archeological discoveries and interest in pre-Renaissance building – the previously despised Gothic architecture of the great cathedrals. Whereas the "Gothick" of Horace Walpole's Strawberry Hill and later Regency style had been a decorative pastiche, the new medievalists set out to recreate consciously the architecture of the past.

They failed. It was inevitable because they could not see that thirteenth-century builders had operated under wildly different social and economic conditions, nor could they acknowledge the anachronistic absurdity of putting an Elizabethan manor house in the middle of a middle-class Victorian suburb. Renaissance architects had always mod-

Interior of University Museum, Oxford, England (1855-60). Deane & Woodward. The architects were personally encouraged by Ruskin, whose influence is clearly seen in the exterior (page 107). Inside all is light and lacy – Neo-Gothic translated into industrial cast-iron tracery, a perfect fusion of historicism and contemporary functionalism.

Royal Albert Bridge, Saltash, Plymouth, England (1853-59). Brunel's best known bridge, it crosses the River Tamar and stands 100ft (30m) above the river.

ified the classical grammar to suit the times; Palladio, Mansart, Kent and the New England architects bear witness to their success. This was not enough for men like A.W.N. Pugin (1812-52) and George Gilbert Scott (1811-78), for whom a total commitment to the past was essential. This movement, the Gothic Revival, was championed in England by the critic John Ruskin (1819-1900) who, during a honeymoon in Italy, fell in love with the early buildings of Venice. This resulted in *The Stones of Venice* (1851-53), one of the most influential works of its time, both at home and abroad. It changed the face of Britain. The Venetian arches and fruiting capitals of surburban houses stem directly from his book, however much he later deplored the way his careful illustrations had been debased by speculative builders.

Grand Magasin du Printemp, Paris *(1881-89). The interior cornice and rise of the central dome in an iron-built French department store.*

England was by no means alone in returning to the past: the movement was alive in Europe, particularly in Germany and Austria. Classical architecture held its own, popular with the establishment in every country. Queen Victoria, in spite of the new Gothic Houses of Parliament, chose Italianate for her house on the Isle of Wight. There was much popular controversy and what has come to be known as the "Battle of the Styles" raged for most of the nineteenth century. However, a reaction set in against the severities of the revival.

In England, William Morris (1834-96), taking a generally Ruskinian line, liberated design with his workshop-biased approach to a simpler, if still medieval, architecture. To him the Great Exhibition of 1851 had been a tawdry disaster. The new style, "Arts and Crafts," developed eventually into a form of "Art Nouveau," a new movement which Victor Horta (1861-1947) had initiated in Brussels.

Architecture in the USA

All this time the United States was growing in prosperity and intellectual self confidence. A new and wholly American architecture emerged, notably in the robust mid-West which was free of European ties and the conservatism of New England. From Chicago came the first great commercial buildings of Louis Sullivan (1856-1924). Frank Lloyd Wright (1869-1959) established his practice in the expanding suburbs of Oak Park, Chicago producing a spectacular collection of houses of exceptional individuality and talent. American architecture became of international importance.

In all the countries of the West, forces were combining to form the "New Architecture." Few were quite confident about the form this would eventually take, but the approach of the new century excited the more revolutionary architects to didactic theories and manifestoes. The United States had made its own contributions with the skyscraper, but the hard core of the new architecture was in the hands of Horta in Belgium, and Otto Wagner (1841-1918) in Austria. By now improved communications replaced the slow transmission of ideas from frontier to frontier. An exhibition of Wright's work in Germany, or Charles Rennie Mackintosh's in Austria could result in overnight fame and influence. The currency of architecture accelerated with cheap printing and the camera wielded an unsuspected influence.

In Britain, the turn of the century saw a reaction to the Victorian, only in the earnest vernacular of Charles Voysey (1857-1941) and Sir Edwin Lutyens (1869-1944). In Europe, Art Nouveau died almost still born. The public had always viewed it with suspicion, associating it with bohemian aestheticism. Its formal licence prevented easy adaptation to standardized building components such as doorways and windows. Ornament for its own sake seemed suddenly less relevant. Alfred Loos (1870-1933) in Austria went further. "Ornament is Crime," he said, and the foundations of true Modernism and the International Style were laid.

CAST-IRON STRUCTURES

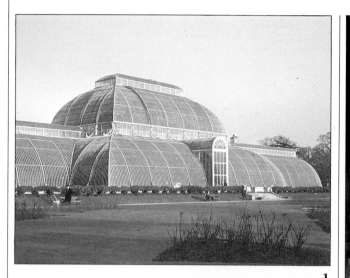

1

1. Palm House, Kew, England *(1844). Burton brought constructional expertise to his buildings. He never wavered from the classical tradition at a time of much stylistic controversy. Among his semi-engineering achievements (with R. Turner), this vast palm house at Kew is both lovely and functional.*

2

2. Bibliothèque National, Paris *(1862-68). Labrouste. The columns supporting the domes on pendentives seem impossibly slender, adding to the fantasy of the spectacular interior. Lightweight terracotta and cast iron make this fragile structure possible, another indication of the direction architecture was taking.*

3. Paddington Station, London *(1852). Brunel. Brunel was the pioneer designer of bridges, ships and railway stations. The Industrial Revolution is elegantly displayed in this curved span of steel trusses supported on cast-iron columns.*

3

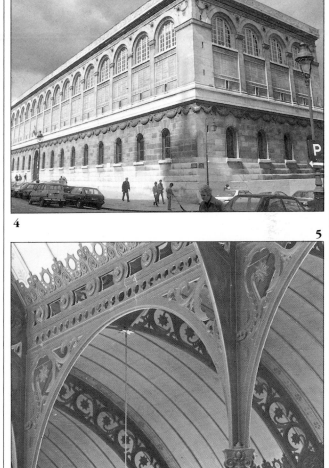

4

5

4/5. Bibliothèque Ste Geneviève, Paris *(1845-50). Henri Labrouste (1801-75). At first sight this appears to be an unexceptional Neo-Classical building. Its function as a library, however, is expressed by the names of authors, inscribed on the exterior panels, who are represented on the shelves within. The treatment of the* *upper stories hints at the open-plan inside, a foretaste of the modern movement. Most architects concealed the ironwork in their buildings behind masonry or plaster. Labrouste was among the first to flaunt the material for its own aesthetic. Here the structural members are highly decorated, with striking effect.*

ENGINEERING IN ARCHITECTURE

1. Dixon Mills, Carlisle, England *(1836). Nothing illustrates better the triumph and oppression of the Industrial Revolution than these vast mills in England's north.*

2. Clifton Suspension Bridge, Bristol, England *(1830-59). Brunel. A magnificent early bridge across the Avon Gorge. Even the massive Egyptian-like pylons are original, owing little to contemporary architecture.*

3

4

5

3. Les Halles, Paris *(1854-66). Victor Balthard (1805-74). An experimental and successful building in cast iron and glass, with wood infilling. This important work has since been destroyed and the site redeveloped.*

4. Kings Cross Station, London *(1852). Lewis & Joseph Cubitt. Kings Cross is significant because, unlike most railway termini of its time, the front facade expressed exactly the profile and engineering structure of the train sheds behind. The effect of the large self-supporting brick arches has been lost with recent building in front of the station.*

5. Gare du Nord, Paris *(1863). J.I. Hittorf (1792-1867). While not as starkly functional as Kings Cross, the Gare du Nord certainly expresses the iron sheds behind, at the same time transforming the facade into a free interpretation of the Roman baths of Caracalla.*

1. Garabit Viaduct, Cantal, France *(1880). Gustave Eiffel (1832-1923). Eiffel was an engineer, specializing in bridges. This one, with a span of 545ft (165m) was a remarkable achievement for the time, made up of huge arches braced with trussed beams. He used lightweight, pre-formed sections which were both cheap and easy to assemble.*

2. Eiffel Tower, Paris *(1889). The famous monument by which Eiffel will forever be known. Built for the Paris Exhibition of 1889, it was the tallest structure at that time at 1010ft (300m). Opinion varies as to its beauty, but most have come to accept it as an essential ingredient of the Paris skyline.*

3. Galleria Vittorio Emanuelle, Milan, Italy *(1865). Guiseppe Mengoni (1829-77). An early shopping precinct of enormous brio and style. The heavy classical architecture is a little incongruous against the modern-looking steelwork.*

4. St Katherine's Docks, London *(1825). Telford. Like many fellow Scotsmen, Telford was virtually self taught. He became a county surveyor and went on to design many civil projects such as bridges, roads, piers, canals and even churches. His architecture is always functional, like this London dock, yet it is by no means without a sense of proportion and unpretentious style.*

2

3

4

GOTHIC

1. Woodbridge Lodge, Suffolk, England (c 1800). This extraordinary folly was a lodge to a country house. In 1801, the owner employed Henry Hakewell to gothicize Rendlesham Hall and it is likely the architect was also responsible for this dotty cottage, contrived under a kind of medieval market cross. However crazy, the absence of such extravaganzas in recent years must be counted our loss.

2. Folly Tower, Painshill Park, Surrey, England (1770). In 1738 Charles Hamilton returned from the Grand Tour of Europe and started to create one of the great eighteenth-century landscape gardens on a virgin hilltop. The delights include this folly tower, a Gothic tent, Chinese bridge and a Temple of Bacchus.

3. Rathaus, Vienna, Austria (1872-83). Friedrich Schmidt (1825-91). Schmidt was the most important figure in German Gothicism, and for a while worked in the cathedral workshops in Cologne. His best work is this Vienna Town Hall, in which he combines a Classical symmetry with Neo-Gothic details transplanted from northern Italy.

4

5

4/5. Strawberry Hill, London *(1750-70). In 1747 Horace Walpole bought an ordinary small house on the banks of the Thames and decided to make it extraordinary. With an architect, William Robinson, and advisers including Robert Adam, he started to transform it into Gothic, at that time a much-despised style. Although he believed he was recreating genuine medievalism, the detailing is more of a charming form of the fashionable Rococo. The pretty plaster fan vaults, their ribs gilded, were based on Henry VII's chapel at Westminster Abbey.*

ARTS & CRAFTS

1/2. Red House, Bexley Heath, Kent, England *(1859). Philip Webb (1831-1915). Webb built this house for the designer William Morris in a medieval vernacular style, which nevertheless combined later features such as sash windows – a Dutch import not widely in use until about 1700. The circular windows have no obvious Gothic precedents.*

The interior is more forward looking than the outside, incorporating features which later became the currency of the Arts and Crafts movement. The striking, fitted cupboards with their decorative hinges are by Morris.

1

2

3. Kelmscott Manor, Oxfordshire, England *(16th cent). Altered by William Morris (1871). Morris sympathetically altered and restored this gabled Elizabethan house. This is the quintessential English manor house Morris so much admired, undefiled by any classical pretensions of the Renaissance.*

3

4. Clock House, London
(1879). Norman Shaw (1831-1912). Shaw became the most important domestic architect of his time, veering between Old English and Queen Anne Revival, a style he did much to promote. His town houses were usually in this neo-Renaissance mold, brick with sash windows, bays and oriels.

5. University Museum, Oxford, England *(1855-59). Deane & Woodward. John Ruskin took a great personal interest in this building, especially the details of sculpture and decoration. The exterior betrays no sign of the wonderful glass-roofed interior, page 96.*

6. Conyhurst, Surrey, England *(1885). Webb continued his practice after the Red House with a number of buildings in a "William & Mary" style that hovered between Old English and the Renaissance and in which he clearly felt most comfortable. This country house shows his typically thoughtful and unpretentious hand.*

4

5

6

REVIVALISM

1

2

1. Houses of Parliament, London (1840-60). Charles Barry (1795-1860) & Pugin. Barry, essentially a classical architect, won the rebuilding in a competition. His young assistant, Pugin, a fervent Gothicist, became responsible for most of the interior work which is in the Perpendicular style. The building became influential in establishing the credentials of the Gothic Revival.

2. Albert Memorial, London (1864). Scott. The architecture may be impeccable Gothic but the effect, enhanced by the mosaic decorations, is overwhelmingly High Victorian. Nevertheless, much of the detail is worth study.

3. Law Courts, London (1868-82). G.E. Street (1824-81). A one-time assistant in Scott's office, Street continued a personal and somewhat severe Gothic Revival style. The Law Courts, won in competition in 1866, show how he combined his austere detailing with great freedom of facade treatment, so that the result is never dull and is always impressive.

3

4

4. Royal Pavilion, Brighton, England *(1815-20). Nash. One of the endearing qualities of Nash was his willingness to turn his hand to any style, though an innate Classicism lay beneath all his buildings. This extravaganza, built for the Prince Regent (later George IV) at the then fashionable resort, owes much to Mogul buildings in Delhi, but its silhouette and fantastic multi-style oriental interiors make it one of the great architectural delights.*

5

5. Leighton House, London *(1877-79). Lord Leighton & Aitchison. A Victorian version of Persian architecture. This was the painter Leighton's own house, built at a time when exotic Eastern styles were popular, particularly in interiors. The workmanship and attention to detail make this a rewarding experience.*

6. Oddfellows Building, Devonport, England *(1822-24). J. Foulston (1772-1842). Another popular variation in the early eighteenth century was the Egyptian. The style was unexpectedly suited to transformation, as is shown here, into Regency stucco decoration.*

7. Pagoda, Kew Gardens, England *(1757-62). Chambers' work at Kew, while apparently picturesque and light hearted, shows a serious understanding of oriental forms. This colorful pagoda provides London with one of its most splendid landmarks.*

6

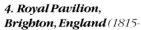

7

AMERICAN STYLES

1

2

1. John Vassal House, Cambridge, USA (1759). A fine New England house. English and Dutch styles predominate, but the clapboard and shutters show the emergence of a national style.

2. Wood House, Long Island, USA. (19th cent). The direct Georgian simplicity of domestic houses had, by mid-century, become more elaborate, even ostentatious. Growing national prosperity saw the building of country houses outside New York for the wealthy business families to spend the summer.

3. Boston Public Library, USA (1888-92). McKim, Mead & White. McKim had worked as an assistant in Richardson's office but remained closer to the work of Norman Shaw in England, favoring a neo-Renaissance style. The Boston Library is based on Labrouste's Ste Geneviève Library (page 99) but has lost something of the excitement of the original in its translation across the Atlantic.

4. Trinity Church, Boston, USA (1873-77). Henry Richardson (1838-86). Richardson was born in Louisiana and went to study in Paris, a background reflected in his architecture in which French and English forms of Romanesque and Gothic combine. Trinity Church, won in competition, is a massive but personal essay in Romanesque, brutally detailed in pink granite and rough ashlar. There is no doubt, however, of the impact it makes in this Boston Square.

3

4

5

5. Newport Casino, Rhode Island, USA (1881-88). McKim, Mead & White. The Richardson influence is apparent in this early work of the celebrated partnership which was to be the dominant East Coast practice of its time. White had just left Richardson's office in the year before this racy casino was erected.

6. Crane Memorial Library, Quincy, Massachusetts, USA (1880-83). Richardson. This rich and impeccably crafted interior must surely be everyone's dream of the perfect library – quiet, secure and hallowed.

6

7

7. State Capitol, Providence, Rhode Island, USA (1900). McKim, Mead & White. A splendid example of colonial Renaissance in the days when state buildings were designed to impress and inspire awe. There are echoes of the grand precedent in Washington.

EARLY SKYSCRAPERS

1

2

3

5

6

6. Empire State Building, New York (1930). *Shreve, Lamb & Harmon. The skyscraper tower par excellence. For some time the tallest building in the world. Its commercial success, coinciding with the Depression, was for a time in jeopardy. In detail it is dull, but the buttressing of the upper stories and Art Deco Gothic spire are well handled.*

1. Flat-iron Building, New York (1902). *Daniel Burnham (1846-1912). This famous landmark in New York expresses succinctly the plan of its narrow triangular site.*

2. Woolworth Building, New York (1913). *Cass Gilbert (1859-1934). Gilbert strove to impose traditional forms to the skyscraper. Gothic, with its emphasis on the vertical, seemed appropriate, and there is no doubt the Woolworth Tower is one of the best considered of all city skyscrapers. Long out of favor for its architectural "dishonesty," it now enjoys deserved appreciation.*

3. Municipal Building Center, New York (1913). *McKim, Mead & White. Although lively enough in its general modeling, this building exposes one of the great problems of the* skyscraper – what to do with the middle stories. The top and bottom are interesting enough, but in-between is distinctly arid.

4. Wrigley Building, Chicago, USA (1921). *Graham, Anderson, Probst & White. The criticism of unrelieved central stories applies to this commercial building, though the windows are well proportioned.*

5. Carbide & Carbon Building, Chicago, USA (1929). *Burnham Brothers. The concept of skyscraper as tower has much to be said for it, at least for the person in the street, and its replacement by slabs and blocks has ruined many skylines. Once again commercial considerations have robbed us of what is now a virtually extinct glory.*

4

THE CHICAGO SCHOOL

1

2

3

4

1. Auditorium Building, Chicago, USA *(1886-90). Adler & Sullivan. Sullivan returned to Chicago from a brief period of study in Paris and set up a partnership with Dankmar Adler. This, their first major building, brought them instant success. Its load-bearing stone facade owes much to Richardson, carefully tiered in a Renaissance manner to break up its huge mass. The interior decoration is also by Sullivan.*

2. Reliance Building, Chicago, USA *(1890-95). Burnham & Root. A glimpse of the future, anticipating the curtain wall with its large proportion of glass to solid. The modeling of the facade is particularly successful. Chicago is a windy city and the internal bracing took account of this.*

3. Gage Building, Chicago, USA *(1898). Holabird & Roche. Facade by Sullivan. The familiar sinuous decorations are treated almost like capitals on the central pilasters.*

4. Fisher Building, Chicago, USA *(1897). Burnham & Root. A skyscraper with applied Classical-Gothic decoration, unusual in Burnham's other Chicago School work. The addition of projecting bays lends a vertical distinction to the facade.*

5

6

5. Carson Pirie Scott Store, Chicago, USA *(1899-1904). Sullivan. Sullivan's personal form of decoration, executed in cast iron, is shown around this entrance to a department store. By comparison, the upper stories of the steel-framed building are plainly treated.*

6. Old Stock Exchange, Chicago, USA *(1894). Adler & Sullivan. Another example of Sullivan's decoration, this time as a carved stone spandrel.*

ART NOUVEAU

1

1. Stained glass, Prague
(c 1900). The Art Nouveau style was officially created in Belgium, but similar and sympathetic work was being carried out all over Europe. This glass is typical of the decorative side of the movement at the turn of the century.

2. Maison du Peuple, Brussels, Belgium *(1896-99). Horta was a genuinely revolutionary architect who turned his back on the whole of the nineteenth-century tradition. In this meeting place for the Belgian Socialist Party, he frankly exposed the structural steelwork to anticipate the cityscape of the twentieth century.*

2

3. Majolica House, Vienna, Austria (1898). Wagner was the founder of the modern Austrian movement and taught as Professor of the Academy. He consciously determined to set aside the past and concentrate on the present. The basic forms of this apartment building are simple, the decorations Art Nouveau – the next step toward an even more severe functionalism.

4. Castel Béranger, Rue de la Fontaine, Paris (1894-98). Hector Guimard (1867-1942). One of the most talented French Art Nouveau designers, famous for his designs for the Paris Métro. This entrance shows his flowing forms in both steel and cast plaster. Eventually the difficulty of resolving rectangular building components within organic shapes brought this movement to a conclusion.

5. Tassel House, Brussels, Belgium (1892-93). Horta. Although Art Nouveau was short lived, its spatial liberation was to become influential in the new Modernism which followed. Horta's decoration was abstract, derived from plant forms; nevertheless, its organic virility is close to Nature in essence and spirit.

1

1/2. Casa Batlló, Barcelona, Spain *(1907). Antonio Gaudi (1852-1926). Gaudi's contribution to architecture is at once brilliant and inimitable. He pursued a solitary path to create a personal form of Art Nouveau long after the style had died out in the rest of Europe. This facade is actually a remodeling of an existing apartment building: whether the strange plastic applications are beautiful or ugly hardly seems an important judgment in the context of this extraordinary building. Everything is in motion, topped by a writhing roof covered with reptilian scales. To look for precedents is in vain: elements of Rococo are there – particularly Spanish and Portuguese – but in the end one can only describe it as "Gaudiesque."*

2

3

SILENCE

4

3/4. School of Art Library, Glasgow, Scotland *(1896-1910). Charles Rennie Mackintosh (1868-1928). This design won the competition for the Glasgow School of Art. The Library is simpler than a first glance might suggest; the vertical elements of the columns and lights provide a lively but not restless interior.*

The outside shows Mackintosh's muscular handling of form which perhaps owes much to traditional Scottish architecture. Continental Art Nouveau, however, shows itself in the subtle treatment of the ironwork in the curved brackets to the second floor.

5. Hill House, Near Glasgow, Scotland *(1903). Mackintosh. Hill House owes much to Voysey in its general outline but the influence of seventeenth-century Scottish laird's houses is even stronger. The surface is "harled," or pebbledashed, in the traditional Scottish manner.*

5

CHAPTER SIX
INTO THE TWENTIETH CENTURY

FUNCTION AND FORM

INTRODUCTION

The end of a century brings with it endless speculation, as if the change from one century to the next exercises some potent influence. Unfortunately, historical periods resist such convenient pigeonholing. The first stirring of what is called International Modern were in the 1880s, a time when artistic reaction to High Victorianism combined with advances in technology. Socially, however, the nineteenth century can be said to have met its conclusive end in the nightmare of the First World War. After that, everything changed.

If Modernism in architecture conjures up a picture, it is the white Cubist style which developed in Germany and Austria in the early 1900s, spreading to Holland in the movement known as De Stijl, before reaching the rest of Europe and the United States. Unlike most previous styles, it never caught on with the general public. Indeed so limited was its influence, that it was almost completely ignored except by its intellectual devotees. However, the repercussions of the Modern movement could no longer be ignored with the rebuilding of Europe after the Second World War.

Functionalism

It is not easy to say which was the first truly modern building, though the Steiner House in Vienna by Adolph Loos has as good a claim as any, though buildings by Behrens, Horta and Perret are credible runners-up. There followed at once a number of the familiar white boxes with simple rectangular openings placed where they suited the plan rather than the elevation. That was the theory at least, though the treatment of many of the De Stijl facades clearly owe their careful arrangement to the abstract theories of painters like Mondrian. In other words, as was to happen so often later, elaborate theories were put forward to justify what were fundamentally aesthetic rather than functional preferences. "Functionalism" was the word. "Form follows function," not the reverse as before. The past was despised – tradition, vernacular, ornament, the Beaux Arts School – all not only unnecessary in the new world but positively dishonest. But hadn't something like this been heard before? It was William Morris who had said it, and though his designs were different to look at, the reasoning of the two schools was similar in the moral purpose.

When Walter Gropius (1883-1969) designed and became principal of the famous Bauhaus school in Germany, he ran it on strictly Morris principles. Architecture had to be taught as a craft like any other. "Fine Art" was to give way to the humble, if now largely industrialized craftsman. The parallels to early socialism were clear. As in society, every craft was to stand on equal terms with another: in building, no element was of greater or lesser importance than its neighbor. In this way the pretensions and pomp of the old order would wither away and die.

That was the theory. In practice it went rather differently.

Behrens' House, Darmstadt, Germany
(1900). Behrens. The architect's own house was part of a whole scheme of building commissioned by the Grand Duke of Hesse as part of an artists' colony. It is one of his first houses and reflects his Art Nouveau style, which he soon abandoned.

In the first place ordinary people didn't like International Modern very much, and with familiarity seemed to like it less and less. Secondly, it was never taken up by any group except the intellectual. The aristocracy thought it common. Hitler and Mussolini chose Neo-Classical monuments to reflect past glories and advance their own. British imperialism was nicely served by Sir Edwin Lutyens, and the middle classes felt safer in their watered down vernacular. In the United States it was much the same, modern buildings being limited to city centers and industrial estates. Clients happy to accept the prairie houses of Frank Lloyd Wright were not yet ready for a Loos or Rietveld.

To be accepted universally a style had to be "smart," and it was only smart in the very limited intellectual circles so brilliantly pilloried by the English cartoonist Osbert Lancaster. Lancaster created a wonderful couple; the male, a heavy, bearded man clad in tweeds and smoking a pipe, pontificates while his female counterpart idles on uncomfortable plywood furniture, and smokes from a long cigarette holder. Their prospect is bleak – large picture windows looking out onto nothing much from bare rooms brightened only by cacti and abstract sculpture. Perhaps the earnestness of the movement in Anglo-Saxon countries was its undoing. In Scandinavia they managed it better, for there it merged with an enlightened socialism and long-standing vernacular to produce a version of Modernism which was not only to influence American and British design, but managed to survive as the popular, even established style for the rest of the twentieth century.

INTRODUCTION

Mies and Le Corbusier

It was, however, in Germany and France that the two great masters of the movement were born – Ludwig Mies Van Der Rohe (1886-1969) and Charles-Edouard Jeanneret (1887-1966), self-styled Le Corbusier.

Mies and Le Corbusier were radically opposed in temperament and outlook, however committed both were in principle to the new architecture. Of the two, Le Corbusier had, at least at first, the greater influence. This was due in a large part to indefatigable self promotion through his publications. The first and perhaps most established of these was his *Vers une Architecture*, published in 1923 and shortly afterwards in English under the title *Towards a New Architecture*. In this work, the beliefs which were to remain constant all his life were laid down. Among these was his wish to liberate the building from its site, a technique now possible with reinforced concrete, by putting the building on stilts, or pilotis as they came to be known. Another freedom was now possible on both plan and elevation. Load-bearing

Swiss House, Cite Universitaire, Paris (1930-32). Le Corbusier. One of the pre-war Le Corbusier buildings which established his reputation, it stands out in a fairly ordinary campus of traditional buildings.

walls could be dispensed with in framed buildings; lightweight partitions now formed the room dividers. In the same way openings could be of any shape, allowing windows to be long and uninterrupted, a form impossible in traditional load-bearing construction. These features can all be seen in the famous Villa Savoye, a classic example of his early style.

Like many theorists, what Le Corbusier said was strictly true, but time has shown that the concrete techniques he advocated have failed to be as cheap as traditional methods and except in high-rise buildings, most houses of today have reverted to constructional methods which would be familiar to the Victorians.

Perhaps the lesson to be learnt is that great architecture rarely comes cheap. This was also true of Mies Van Der Rohe. Le Corbusier was essentially a romantic, a sculptor who rationalized his architectural sculpture by a complicated set of self-imposed rules of proportion, based on the Greek "Golden Section," which he called the Modulor. For many years Le Corbusier was to write more books than he was able

Christian Science Church, Berkeley, California, USA (1912). Bernard Maybeck (1862-1937). An original style, built largely in wood, this mixture of West coast vernacular and Gothic was influential in the San Francisco Bay area.

to put into buildings, and his greatest period began after World War Two. Mies on the other hand set out deliberately to suppress personality and produce a refined architecture of reduction, perfectly expressed in his famous remark "Less is more." His other guiding maxim was "Reason is the first principal of all human work," a saying he discovered in the writings of St Thomas Aquinas. In his architecture the form *is* the structure; he never tried to force structure into a preconceived form.

This eventually led to some extremes of structural expression, hard to justify under any grounds other than sheer aesthetics; nevertheless his unswerving consistency of purpose has been one of the most impressive contributions to twentieth-century architecture. In 1933, after three years as head of the Bauhaus, he closed it down in protest against Hitler, and in 1938 emigrated to the United States where his career and influence gathered momentum and influence.

Art Deco

Meanwhile, everyday architecture largely continued the dying traditions of the previous century. Housing in Britain was almost untouched by the International Style, its influence surviving in a handful of expensive suburban houses in London or in scattered villas in the Home Counties. Its mark on speculative housing can be seen here and there in groups of flat-roofed, semi-detached houses along surburban highways on the outskirts of cities.

The only truly popular style – much frowned on by hard-line Modernists – was that known as Art Deco, a title more in general use today than at the time. Art Deco was the style of the Jazz Age and derived from a Paris exhibition of decorative art held in 1925. It was Modernism without polemics, a style which owed much to industrial styling, like motor cars, but in which decoration was no longer a crime.

In France, where it was born and flourished, the Musée de l'Art Moderne provides a fascinating example, and in the USA its most famous landmark is the Chrysler Building. In Britain the style was considered suitable for cinemas, restaurants and factories. It was as if no really serious architect could employ it wholeheartedly for anything but purely commercial or entertainment purposes. Its re-emergence in the 1970s as inspiration for another school is perhaps a significant comment on our own times.

Looking back over the years between 1900 and 1940, a great confusion emerges, a confusion reflected in society and all the other arts. The struggles arose out of a genuine conflict between culture and classes. Nothing in architecture today represents quite the same gulf between buildings such as Castle Drogo by Lutyens, and the Steiner House by Adolf Loos, both built in 1911.

Today's cultural divisions, by contrast, seem to be almost wilfully self imposed, a kind of game played without conviction to nourish the passion for novelty and self entertainment. This is a theme and phenomenon to be examined in the final chapter.

Castle Drogo, Devonshire, England (1910-30). Lutyens. *One of the last great English country houses in the grand style although it represents only a part of the original design. It is meticulously constructed from tough local granite.*

EARLY FRANK LLOYD WRIGHT

1

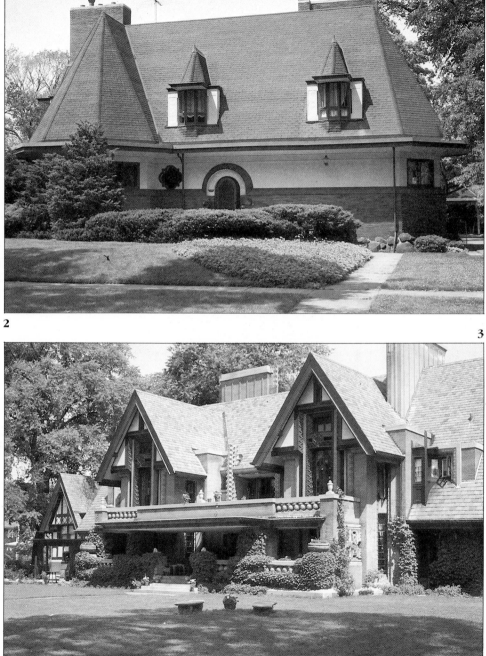

2

3

1. Walter Gale House, Oak Park, Chicago, USA *(1893). Wright. In 1892 Wright left the Sullivan office and set up in practice by himself. There followed in quick succession a number of suburban houses of extraordinary variety and talent. This early example employs features stemming from traditional American domestic architecture but transformed by Wright's personal treatment.*

2. Chauncey Williams House, River Forest, Illinois, USA *(1895). Wright has set an enormous French roof, with picturesque dormers, above a horizontal floor in this surprising house from the Prairie School design book.*

3. Moore House, Oak Park, Chicago, USA *(1895). In this house (remodeled in 1924), the mature Wright is already evident. Elements from his early Chicago houses are here subordinated to a sculptural composition of striking subtlety and character. Its very individuality defies imitation.*

4

5

6

7

4/5. Unity Church, Chicago, USA (1906). Wright. Plain reinforced concrete, with a decorative pebbledash finish, was the material used for this small but monumental church. The Aztec-like columns and wide overhanging eaves were to become features of Wright's style over many years.

Inside, the severe architecture is relieved by simple geometrical patterns, reminiscent of Mackintosh's work in Glasgow of about the same time. Light fittings and furniture are all successfully integrated.

6/7. Imperial Hotel, Tokyo, Japan (1916-22). Wright. Some of the features of the Unity Church can be seen after a ten-year refinement. This was one of Wright's masterpieces, a building of immense spatial and textural surprises. Though the frame structure saved it in the devastating earthquake of 1923, it was demolished in the 1960s to make way for more, and infinitely less rewarding, hotel accommodation. The interior view only hints at the quality of the layout. The public areas flowed into one another in a succession of different volumes and ceiling heights; a guest's procession was like a tour through a piece of abstract sculpture.

BAUHAUS

1

1 AEG Factory, Berlin, Germany *(1909). Peter Behrens (1868-1940). Behrens started his career as an exponent of Art Nouveau. By the time he had been appointed as architect to the electrical firm of AEG, he had thrown off all decorative detailing, and in this turbine factory used poured concrete and steel more frankly expressed than it had been before except in pure engineering. His natural feeling for form gives the impression that he would be a master in any style.*

2. Siemensstadt Housing, Berlin, Germany *(1929). Gropius. Unadulterated Modernism. This was the style which Gropius was to employ for most of his life until a weakening of resolve overtook the spirit during his last years.*

3. Haus, Darmstadt, Germany
(1901). J. M. Olbrich (1867-1908). Olbrich was another architect with a claim to be the first Modernist, and if this is upheld, some credit is also due to Mackintosh whose influence is surely behind this doorway. Olbrich died relatively young, but his influence on architects such as Behrens was significant.

2

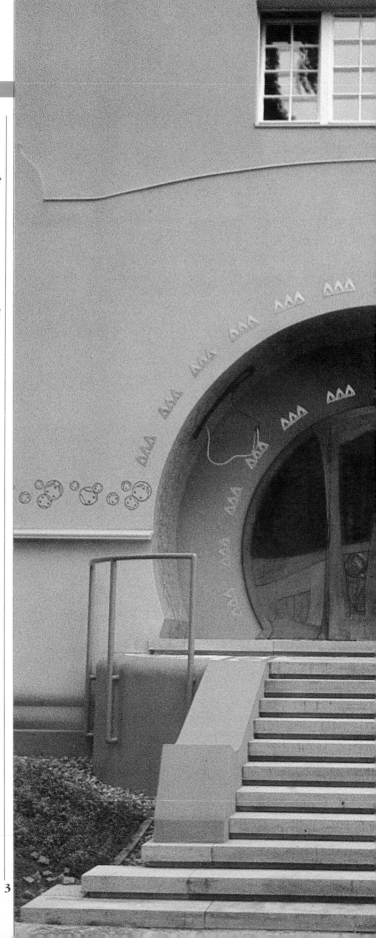

3

4

5

4/5. Bauhaus Buildings, Dessau, Germany *(1926). Gropius. In 1925 Gropius was commissioned to remodel the Bauhaus and become its principal. He was also commissioned to design a number of houses for the teaching staff. The result was a milestone in design teaching, for the school was a combination of craft workshop and fine-art studio with architecture as the link.*

The classroom block is in simple black and white, the precursor of many post-war schools all over Europe.

The workshops are noticeably more industrial, particularly in their window treatment. The square-paneled metal windows are typical of mass-produced industrial units.

EXPRESSIONISM

1

1. Einstein Tower, Potsdam, East Germany (1921). Eric Mendelsohn (1887-1953). This is the most famous Expressionist building of the Modern movement, the work of an architect who almost immediately reverted to the strict geometry of his contemporaries. Originally intended to be cast in reinforced concrete to display the plastic qualities of that material, technical difficulties led it to be largely built in rendered brick. The link between Modernism and Art Nouveau could hardly be better illustrated.

2

3

2/3. Chile Shipping Office, Hamburg, West Germany (1923). Fritz Höger (1877-1949). Among the notable high buildings in Germany of the twenties — by no means a skyscraper by American standards — is this brick-built city block. Making the most of its sharp, angled site, the corner is aggressively treated like the prow of some huge ship, further accentuated by the overhang of the cornice.

With such decorative invention as this, part Gothic, part Art Nouveau, it is impossible not to wonder what other paths modern architecture might have taken but for the overriding domination of the International Style.

4

5

6

4. Tobacco Factory, Hamburg, West Germany *(1923). Another extraordinary facade by Höger. The extreme emphasis on verticals combined with highly decorative and textured brick work result in an optical effect unique in architecture.*

5. Zaanstraat Flats, Amsterdam *(1917-20). Michel de Klerk (1883-1923). De Klerk was an interesting figure of the "Amsterdam School" where German Expressionism mingled with Art Nouveau and, in this example, revealed unintended echoes of Norman Shaw. This architecture was always humane, sometimes humorous, but its individuality is undeserving of the comparative neglect it has suffered.*

6. Hoechst Dyeworks, Frankfurt, West Germany *(1920-25). Behrens' control of brickwork and form are seen here in this early modern factory and suggest his talents might well have been equally displayed as a traditional classicist.*

DOMESTIC INTERNATIONAL MODERN

2

3

**1. Blacker House,
Pasadena, California, USA**
*(1906). Greene & Greene. The
Greene brothers' practice was
devoted almost entirely to
domestic work, to which they
brought a highly sophisticated
wooden architecture. They
supervised construction with
meticulous care, selecting
carpenters of proven ability. The
overhanging eaves may recall
Wright, or even the Swiss chalet,
but the essential individuality is
their own.*

**2. Steiner House, Vienna,
Austria** *(1910). Loos was the
hard-line architect of the
Modern movement, to whom
ornament was a "crime." His
influence can be gauged by the
fact that these houses, at the time
highly revolutionary, now look
merely "modern."*

**3. House, Grunewald,
Germany** *(1929).
Mendelsohn. International Style
house, in a garden setting. This
German example is typical of
the architecture many refugees
brought with them to England
and the USA during the years
before the Second World War.*

4

**4. Melnikov's House,
Moscow, USSR** *(1927). A rare
survival from the brief period of
Russian modernism before the
Stalin era. This house was the
architect's own and is made up
of two cylindrical sections
linked by a staircase.*

**5. Lovell Beach House,
Newport Beach, California,
USA** *(1926). R.M. Schindler
(1887-1953). Born in Vienna,
Schindler was taught there by
Otto Wagner before moving to
the USA, where his practice was
principally domestic. This
concrete example shows his
dexterity in handling the
material.*

5

1

DE STIJL GROUP

1

2

3. Juliana School, Hilversum, Holland *(1923). Marinus Dudok (1884-1974). In contrast with the International Modernism of Rietveld, Dudok cannot be easily categorized. He was a designer with a very personal treatment of roof, wall and glazing in which asymmetrical elements are combined with force and subtlety.*

4. Ruysdael School, Hilversum, Holland *(1920). Dudok. The elements of steep roof, plain walls and strongly defined glazing have been satisfactorily combined. The look is almost vernacular, turning its back resolutely on De Stijl modernism, yet at the same time clearly of its century.*

3

4

1/2. Schroeder House, Utrecht, Holland *(1924). Gerrit Rietveld (1888-1964). A furniture designer and cabinet maker by training, Rietveld became a member of the modernist De Stijl group, whose members were trying to bring unity in the arts, expressed in simple planes and volumes. The influence of the abstract painter Mondrian and French Cubism can be seen in this house.*

The detail is an abstract painting turned into architecture. Only with reinforced concrete could such fragile panels and cantilevered balconies be realized, exploiting a technology which was still in its infancy.

5. Open Air School, Amsterdam, Holland (1930-32). Johannes Duiker (1890-1935). Another member of the De Stijl group. This functional treatment of white concrete with simple fenestration remained internationally influential until after the Second World War.

5

STEEL & GLASS

1

1. German Pavilion for the Barcelona Exhibition (reconstruction) *(1929).*
Mies van der Rohe. With Mies van der Rohe, the second phase of the Modern Movement began. Like the De Stijl group, the basic abstract foundation is apparent, but now infinitely more sophisticated. The extreme simplicity is deceptive: each element has been calculated with immense attention and to the highest standard.

2. Tugendhat House, Brno, Czechoslovakia *(1930). Mies van der Rohe. This influential house pioneered the "open plan." The outside of the house demonstrates the simple geometry of the structure with large cantilevers and floor-to-ceiling windows. Mies liked to create a simple rectangular envelope in which screen walls provided strictly non-loadbearing, and often, movable partitions.*

2

3

4

5

3. Fagus Shoe Factory, Alfed-an-der-Liene, Germany *(1911-14). Gropius & Meyer. This factory created something of a sensation. Gropius was among the first to define the functional aesthetic and put it into direct and attractive practice. The idea that corners should have no visible supports was entirely new.*

4. Van Nelle Factory, Rotterdam, Holland *(1928-30). Brinkman & van der Vlught. This Dutch chocolate factory may look unexceptional today but in its time it was recognized as one of the finest modern industrial buildings. It was also one of the first buildings in which glass curtain walling was used.*

5. Johnson Wax Building, Racine, Wisconsin, USA *(1936-39). Wright. Wright's work for the Johnson Wax Company resulted in this highly sophisticated building, unique in any commercial sphere. The laboratory tower (added 1949-51), cantilevered from a central core, has glazing made of glass rods to accommodate the rounded corners.*

REINFORCED CONCRETE

1. 25 Rue Franklin, Paris
(1903). Auguste Perret (1874-1954). One of the most important figures of modern French architecture, Perret had a profound faith that reinforced concrete was to be the material of the future. This view shows the underlying classicism of his architectural grammar combined with the new structural techniques. The glazed walls are not loadbearing.

2. Stadium, Florence, Italy
(1930-32). Pier Luigi Nervi. One of the most inventive engineers with a strong sense of the aesthetic possibilities of reinforced concrete. In his long career Nervi has produced some notable forms in this material, including the stadium for the Rome Olympics.

3. Notre Dame de Raincy, Paris *(1922-23). Perret. In this elegant church the concrete is exposed just as it left the shuttering, or mold. This raw use of the material has become one of the obsessions of the Modern movement, usually with more success in countries where it can be protected from the ravages of climate. Stained glass windows extend from floor to ceiling.*

1

2

3

4

5

4. Royal Horticultural Society Hall, London *(1923). A fine no-nonsense exhibition hall. The elegant parabolic arches are strengthened, both visually and structurally, by overhanging horizontal beams. Round skylights along the ridge complete the composition.*

5. Bauhaus, Dessau, Germany *(1926). Gropius. One of the most famous buildings of the Modern Movement, not merely on account of its architecture but as a revolutionary workshop where architecture was taught in the same way as other crafts. The complex consisted of a school, a hostel and a workshop. Its designer and Principal, Gropius, was following in the Morris tradition, however different the results may look. After a brief period, the art school was taken over under the Hitler regime and much of the old vitality vanished.*

6. Exhibition Hall, Turin, Italy *(1948). Pier Luigi Nervi (1891-1979). The leading Italian engineer contrived a magnificent span of 240ft (73m) in a series of ribbed concrete sections which incorporate clerestory roof lighting for this large hall.*

BRITISH URBAN ARCHITECTURE

1

2

3

4

1. Housing, Silver End, Essex, England (1927). Thomas Tait (1882-1954). The Modern Movement in England. It was almost de rigeur to build modern houses in concrete or rendered brickwork. The new steel windows were also an essential part. The faintly Art Deco balcony railing suggests an alien contemporary intrusion, one which persisted in the post-war architecture of the Festival of Britain.

2. High and Over, Amersham, England (1929). A.D. Connell. One of the most sensitive and sculptural houses of its time. The use of curves added relief to the form and declared the new plasticity afforded by concrete technology.

3. 64 Old Church Street, Chelsea, London (1936). Mendelsohn & Chermayeff. A restrained town house. The exaggerated horizontality of the first floor forms a long podium for the simpler treatment of the upper story.

4. Highpoint I, Highgate, London (1933). Berthold Lubetkin (b 1901). A pre-war immigrant who was highly influential in English architecture, Lubetkin led a group of architects calling themselves Tecton. These luxury houses, one of two adjacent blocks, have unusual flat plans. The unorthodox concrete construction was handled by the engineer Ove Arup.

5. Bounds Green Station, England (1933). Adams, Holden & Pearson. Charles Holden was the key figure in the partnership which was responsible for more than 30 London Underground Stations. Never a thorough-going Modernist – he had trained under the Arts & Crafts architect, Ashbee – Holden nevertheless developed what might be called Neo-Classical Modernism in which greatly simplified classical elements were employed. His handling of brickwork with stone was always interesting and often magnificent.

6. Sun House, London (1936). Maxwell Fry (b 1899). Skilful English practitioner of the Bauhaus style, as shown in this assured example in Hampstead. The house has reinforced concrete walls, steel columns to support the balconies and extensive glazing.

5

6

TOWN PLANNING

1

2

3

4

1. Bedford Park, London
(1875). Norman Shaw (1831-1912) & others. Shaw was asked to draw up a layout for land to the west of London and the result was one of the first garden suburbs. Shaw designed some of the buildings himself, including the church. Other architects were responsible for the housing.

2. Hampstead Garden Suburb, London *(1907-15). The success of Bedford Park led to similar developments elsewhere. Forerunners to the later "New Towns," the lack of any industry or commerce confirms their suburban status. Architecturally Hampstead is Queen Anne Vernacular, and very soundly built – dull but decent. There is work by Lutyens here.*

3. Letchworth Garden City, Hertfordshire, England
(1903-6). Parker & Unwin. The first Garden City. Unwin, who started life as an engineer, was much influenced by Ebenezer Howard, whose ideas for new towns he put into practice. The strongly vernacular gables are appropriate to their rural setting, but the empty verges and bald lawns pose a problem unaddressed by most new towns ever since.

4. Port Sunlight, Merseyside, England
(1911). Named after the product that made a fortune for its founders, Lever Brothers, this was one of the first garden towns built specifically for industrial workers. North Country Elizabethan has been added to the vernacular ingredients.

5

6

5. Plymouth, England
(1944-52). Paton, Watson & Abercrombie. An example of British post-war reconstruction. The contrast with earlier new towns is clear in this continental-style civic center. The introduction of municipal lawns to mitigate rigid axial planning cannot be judged a successful contribution to city design.

6. Town Center, Le Havre, France *(1945-61). Perret. Wide boulevards and Beaux Arts planning do not compensate for monotonous and repetitive architecture in the reconstruction of the war-damaged port.*

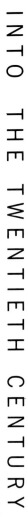

HOUSING

1

1. Double House, Stuttgart, West Germany *(1927). Le Corbusier. Even in this simple twin house – one dare hardly call it a semi-detached – Le Corbusier's individuality is evident in every detail. The huge concrete facade, with its top terrace canopy, is poised dramatically on the familiar pilotis, which leaves the first floor open, free from its site.*

2. Embassy Court, Brighton, England *(1935). Wells Coates (1895-1958). Modernism did not attract public housing clients in England as it had on the Continent. Most examples of the new architecture were restricted to private developments, like these apartments, or to private houses. Embassy Court is a sophisticated courtyard building, though its great bulk and aggressive horizontality hardly make it a comfortable intrusion among its Regency neighbors.*

2

3. Houses, Los Angeles, USA *(1919, since restored). Irving Gill (1870-1936). Gill is an interesting architect. At first sight his work seems to stem directly from Europe, but in fact he developed his own Modernism from the Spanish mission traditions of simple mud and plaster walls, clear cut and whitewashed. His interiors are more reminiscent of Voysey than Loos or Gropius.*

4. Terrace housing, Utrecht, Holland *(1930). Rietveld & Schroder. While lacking the unequivocal simplicity of Mies housing, these Dutch terraces bear all the hallmarks of their affiliation – flat roofs, large windows and plain white wall surfaces.*

3

4

5. Wesissenhof Estate, Stuttgart, West Germany *(1927). Mies van der Robe. The early housing of Gropius, Mies and Le Corbusier is strikingly similar, a genuinely International Style which only Gropius was to pursue into later life. These apartments by Mies provide a crisp example of this early approach whose simplicity is deceptive.*

5

POLITICAL ARCHITECTURE

1. Luitpold Arena, Nuremburg, West Germany *(1935). Albert Speer (1905-81). Speer is better known as Hitler's architect in which profession he continued the monumental Neo-Classical tradition started by Schinkel. The autocracies of fascism and communism flirted with the Modern movement before retreating into Classicism, which they presumably felt expressed more appropriately the permanence and stability of their regimes.*

1

2

2. Casa del Popolo, Como, Italy *(1932-36). Terragni & Lingari. A "People's house" which was originally known as the Casa Fascio. Guiseppe Terragni (1904-42) was a member of Gruppo 7, a group of rationalist artists who revolted against the traditional styles and found a positive environment in the early days of* *Italian national socialism. Despite distrusting Mussolini's politics, and arousing hostility themselves, they nevertheless welcomed the chance to reject historical styles. Now overtaken by intervening fashions, this building remains a crisp example of the early International movement.*

3. Lomonosov University, Moscow, USSR *(1949-53). By 1932, it was clear that, under Stalin, the state-enforced style was to be Neo-Classical; Constructivism was purged along with the political enemies of the state. This university skyscraper, which was designed by a committee of architects, aroused derision from Western architects when it was built. If its treatment, ironically recalling the New York skyline, deserves some respect, the sheer size and monotony of the whole make it a dismal alternative to the traditional campus.*

3

4. Tatlin Tower, London *(1971 reconstruction). Cross & Dixon. Vladimir Tatlin (1885-1953) was an exponent of a movement in Russia known as Constructivism. He built a model for this tower in wood and glass as a monument to the Third International. His avant-garde public display was not received favorably by the Communist leadership who preferred a more realistic, classical approach. The tower became a symbol of the anti-art movement and was adopted by other movements at the time, such as the Dadaists.*

Not surprisingly the ambitious project was never built; it was designed to stand some 1500ft (454m) high across a wide river and to contain suspended buildings at various levels of the double spiral of interlacing girders.

ART DECO

1

2

1/2. Derry & Toms Store, London *(1933). Bronze panels by Bernard George. Well-mannered Art Deco. These doors go to show just how much has been lost in entrance architecture since World War II. The influence here is strictly Classical; Greek forms are reduced to symbols. The sculpture is of a high quality, as seen in both the frieze and screen, yet a little vulgarity does, after all, seem an essential ingredient to this commercial style. The bronze frieze has a design of deer and birds, common themes for the period.*

3. Shop Front, Paris *(c 1926). The true Art Deco Style, in its birthplace, Paris. Graphics played an important part in the style, as did streamline decoration, often applied in relief as in the frieze above and display windows.*

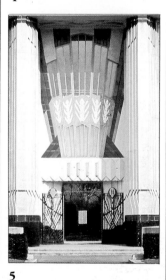

3

4

5

6

4/5. Hoover Factory, Middlesex, England *(1932-35). Wallis Gilbert & Partners. In England Art Deco was generally restricted to commercial and entertainment architecture. The style was popular with the young of the twenties for interiors but their elders tended to look on it as common and prefer traditional designs. No such inhibitions restrained this factory, as can be seen in the uninhibited entrance doors. To the side are vestigial columns or pilasters, so jazzed up as to be barely recognizable, but seeming to descend from Egyptian rather than Greek sources.*

6 Hollyhock House, Los Angeles, USA *(1917-20). Wright. Strictly speaking this house has no place among Art Deco buildings, particularly from its early date, but the parallels are fascinating. Wright's abstract decorations, with their Aztec echoes, are here applied in the same way as jazz patterns were to be used a few years later in Europe. The house is made of poured concrete.*

7. Chrysler Building, New York (1929). William van Alen (1882-1954). It is now considered permissable for architects to admire this building, long considered a piece of kitsch unworthy of critical attention. Although the lower part of the tower is monotonous, the sculptural treatment of the top deserves praise. How many other architects have crowned their buildings with such aplomb?

CHAPTER SEVEN

THE MODERN ERA

FROM INTERNATIONAL TO POST MODERNISM

INTRODUCTION

If the First World War changed society by its fruitless slaughter and rise of Communism, the end of the Second World War saw a more subtle revolution, involving too the changing face of architecture. In 1918, the battlefront was largely limited to a devastated strip dividing France and Germany: in 1945, half of Europe was in ruins and the immediate problem in many countries was reconstruction. The devastation had been terrible, bombs had made no architectural distinctions to London, Dresden, Coventry, Warsaw and Cologne. It is therefore hardly surprising that the initial post-war impetus came from the United States and post-Vichy France where Le Corbusier at last managed to put theory into practice in his first Unité d'Habitation in Marseilles (1946-52). In it he incorporated every facet of his vision to create the first self-contained town gathered in a single block. There are 337 apartments in a huge 17-story slab, elevated on pilotis, on a green site and furnished with shops, a nursery school and sports facilities. It is a great building, magnificently conceived and every inch of it designed to his "Modulor" of ideal proportions. It provided the model for almost all high-rise, post-war building, culminating in the now discredited tower blocks of the inner cities. Who was right? What went wrong?

The New Philosophy

Architecture is of all arts the most arrogant. It is publicly inescapable and there is no essential correlation between form and function. In spite of William Morris and Walter Gropius, buildings can be functionally artificial, even callous – witness Blenheim Palace – yet remain great architecture. Le Corbusier, in the Unite, was only doing what other architects had done for centuries; that was to provide buildings to which the inhabitants would have to adapt, the opposite of humanist ideals where there was tenant participation.

The rationale was infectious. In the book *The Modern Flat* by F.R.S. Yorke and Frederick Gibberd (1937), Le Corbusian theories are argued with great plausibility. In it there is an aerial photograph of a typical speculator's suburb, encroaching like a predator to devour the surrounding countryside. Underneath is an anglicized Unité block, standing in parkland studded with lakes and woods. You are invited to choose which is to be preferred – the ugly sprawl, profligate of land, or the orderly town in the air surrounded by green lawns salvaged by the site economy.

The proposition was doubtless oversimplified, but whether the reaction now is oversimplified, only time will tell. To be sure, Le Corbusier and his followers neglected the social side-effects of their doctrinal authoritarianism, yet the basic problem of land use remains unsolved and is more acute today than in the immediate post-war years.

In the United States, Mies was building apartments too, with even greater arrogance and disregard for the tenants than his French contemporary. He built the twin block Lake

__Notre Dame du Haut, Ronchamp, France__ (1950-55). Le Corbusier. Conscientious readers of Le Corbusier's writings might be surprised at this late work which seems contrary to his mechanistic theories. Visitors to this pilgrimage church should ignore earlier propaganda and enjoy this amazing piece of sculpture on its own terms. The rough-cast concrete walls have small, scattered windows set in deep embrasures which create a magical sequence of internal illumination programed by the passage of the sun as it moves around the hilltop site.

Shore Drive apartments on the Chicago waterfront. No balconies were allowed, they might break the geometry of the block, nor were curtains permitted which, subject to individual choice, would be bound to compromise the purity of his facades. Indeed, it was not until a desperate tenant actually fried an egg in August behind his uncurtained window, that blinds – metallic faced and standard – were allowed by the management.

Frank Lloyd Wright

Compared with these architectural authoritarians, the equally authoritarian Frank Lloyd Wright now stands out as a model of humanity, diametrically opposed in principle to his European rivals. Wright believed in individual houses standing in one acre of land – an easy proposition for America in the fifties. At least his buildings were built for people to love and live in, close to the essential nature to which Wright felt they were entitled and on which they were dependent for spiritual well being.

Wright, Mies and Le Corbusier pursued their own paths, gathering supporters but relatively careless of whether they were establishing schools to continue and propagate their theories. The truth is that such men are inimitable: one cannot become a Le Corbusier by designing to his Modulor, or a Mies by building in steel and glass. Possibly of the three, Wright's influence, because so profoundly individual, has been the least disastrous. Le Corbusier has something to answer for, he is behind every tower block in post-war

INTRODUCTION

AT & T Building, New York
*(1986). Johnson. When
Johnson, a committed purist on
his own account, produced this
building (with Burgee), no-one
knew if the Chippendale top was
a joke or not. The influence this
building has had on recent
architecture has been
widespread. The broken
pediment is now a cliche all
over the world. However, like all
good jokes, once is enough!*

Europe, and those who thought that Mies could be imitated on the cheap have been quickly disillusioned. His influence is in many of the tawdry looking schools and factory units of our towns. It is not entirely their fault: one might just as well blame Voysey or Norman Shaw for every speculative villa built between the wars.

The New Architecture

By the 1960s, the second phase of Modernism was over. The best of the young contemporaries had begun to throw off early allegiances and strike out on their own. The United States provided the most propitious field for the new post-war generation, and the attention of the architectural world was first directed there. The list is impressive: Skidmore, Owings and Merrill, Saarinen, Rudolph, Johnson, Pei, Kahn and many others.

The new architecture took fire in countries across the World – Japan, Australia, South America prominent among them. In Europe, the fifties and sixties saw the gradual establishment and acceptance, however grudging, of the Modern movement. Pockets of resistance hung on to older traditions. In England, Raymond Erith stoutly maintained his impeccable Classical convictions, dying a few years too soon to see his dedication recognized and his influence acknowledged and taken up again.

At another level of course, in all Western countries, a bastardized vernacular remained popular with the general public. In England, the respectably dull Neo-Classicism of the thirties declined into "Estates Georgian," with its fiberglass ornaments substituting for the old stone and plaster, or a kind of aerosol vernacular, with surface Elizabethan applied to the facade. Public housing, tied to liberal policies and hard-hearted economics, stayed with the high rise – quick and cheap to build. New towns followed a vaguely Scandinavian line, brick terraces with a scattering of stubby towers to make up required densities.

The sixties saw a curious restatement of Modernism manifested in the style known as New Brutalism. The Hunstanton School in Norfolk by Peter and Alison Smithson gave the movement its impetus in a building where everything was frankly exposed. Not only structure became part of form, but the services, the ducts, pipes and conduits as well. A decade or so later this aesthetic became the more sophisticated "High Tech." Whatever its merits, High Tech is a genuinely new and individual style. It differs from Brutalism by a light heartedness suggested by Pop Art and commercial styling: perhaps it is nearer the spirit of Art Deco than the pastiche of that style that re-emerged in the 1970s.

The death of the Modern movement has been wittily put by one writer as 3.32pm on July 15th 1972, the moment in which Yamasaki's housing slabs in St Louis were blown up after persistent vandalism had made them unfit for habitation. Architects might retort that this is more a social com-

USA Pavilion, Montreal Expo, Canada (1967). *Buckminster Fuller (1895-1987). The geodesic dome is an innovative structure which can be used as a cover against the weather. This one is made from lightweight tube steel with acrylic panels.*

mentary than a criticism of design, and it is true that a rich man's penthouse is a poor man's tower block. Nevertheless, hostile public reaction has put architects on the defensive and it is unsurprising to find that they have run in different directions to take cover, hiding under the guise of irony, eclecticism or pop culture. It is no longer good form to be too serious: perhaps the very fragility of our continued survival on this planet is too solemn to face. Popular confidence in politicians to provide a brave new world is now no stronger than in architects to provide a better environment.

Post Modernism

Architecture's loss of confidence in the Modern movement has led to the spirit – it can hardly be called a style – known as Post Modernism. This rose simultaneously in several countries, but with most publicity in the USA, the birthplace of Pop Art and West Coast libertarianism

There is much in this architecture to enjoy, and no Ruskin or Gropius has emerged to wag a finger, even if it were to be heeded any longer. The public failure of modern architecture has at least forced architects to turn a critical eye inwards on themselves. They can no longer impose alien environments. If they do, the results are vandalism or prettification. The first change in most sold-off state housing is to the front door: the desire for individuality, however conformist in itself, has not yet been squashed.

Post Modernists in their different ways have found it easier to ride the punches. "If you can't beat them join them," may not be much of a slogan but it is better than demolition. They have joined the pop culture. What the next twist of fashion will be is anybody's guess: perhaps Post Neo-Classicism, but there is no doubt that the familiar swing of action and reaction is still the most potent factor in the history of Art. And there is still life in the Doric temple yet!

FRANK LLOYD WRIGHT

1

2

3

1/2. Falling Water, Bear Run, Pennsylvania, USA (1937-39). Wright. One of the most extraordinary and exciting houses of the century. On a dramatic site above a waterfall in woodland, Wright created a concrete masterpiece to rival anything in this material attempted by his European contemporaries. On the waterfall side, two huge and opposed cantilevered balconies are suspended over the water, the lower one an extension of the living room, separated from it by a light glass screen. The one above is similarly related to sleeping quarters to which it affords a generous terrace.

This cantilever theme extends all around the house; the concrete is rendered a smooth white in contrast with the rough vertical elements in natural stone. The whole result is a complex, but at the same time harmonious sculptural composition.

3. The interior view shows how the structural logic of white horizontal concrete and natural stone piers is integral throughout the house. Note Wright's favorite device of breaking up ceiling heights to create spatial interest and architectural decoration.

4. Taliesin West, Phoenix, Arizona, USA (1938). Frank Lloyd Wright lived at Taliesin in Wisconsin, in a house he designed for himself. In 1938 he built a winter house in the desert of Arizona which he called Taliesin West. For this he used local desert rocks fairly crudely bound together with concrete to form "battered" walls – walls canted inwards to give an impression of strength. The woodwork was equally robust, rough sawn and stained Indian red. The result is a tough, horizontal building complementing its desert backdrop.

5. David Wright House, Phoenix, Arizona, USA (1952). Wright built this desert house for his son, and based it on a circle theme. The entrance approach is up a helical ramp which serves the main rooms – curved on plan – situated on the upper level.

6. Guggenheim Museum, New York (1946-59). Wright's post-war interest in circular buildings and ramps reached its apotheosis in the Guggenheim. The main building consists of a long concrete spiral ramp which combines to form both circulation and gallery functions, lit from above by a central lantern. There has been some criticism of it as a gallery from those who prefer a level floor from which to view paintings, but as an exhilarating space and magical architectural experience, it has no rival.

4

5

7

7. Johnson House, Racine, Wisconsin, USA (1937). A Wright house built around a high central core. The oriental-looking roof lets light in to the living area below by means of continuous clerestories, which throw into relief the textured walls and varying floor levels to produce one of Wright's most dramatic domestic interiors.

6

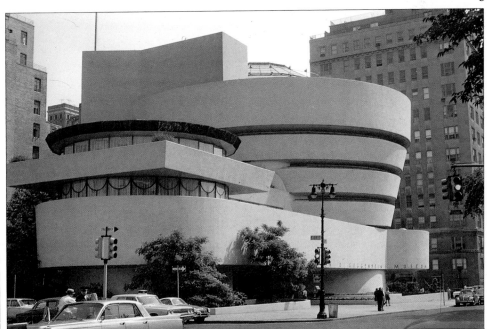

LE CORBUSIER

1

2

3

1. La Roche-Jeanneret House, Paris *(1923). Le Corbusier. A straightforward essay in International Style Cubism – a simple abstract form with no hint of the expressive Mannerism which was to come. This is two buildings joined into one and now houses the Le Corbusier Foundation.*

2. Villa Savoye, Poissy, France *(1929). Le Corbusier published many works on architecture before the opportunity came to put his theories into practice. This house, raised on pilotis, shows his early functionalism at its classically most pure and ordered. The entrance is via a ramp, not the traditional staircase.*

3. Legislative Assembly Chandigarh, India *(1956-70). Le Corbusier was commissioned to design the capital of the Punjab in India. Massive and sculptural, his love of reinforced concrete accentuates the brutal strength of this Parliament building set against the Himalayan foothills.*

4. Unité d'Habitation, Marseilles, France *(1947-52). Le Corbusier. One of the most influential buildings of the twentieth century. It incorporates the architect's dream of multi-story self-contained apartment buildings, standing on their own in the midst of parkland liberated by the small site area of the buildings themselves. On top of the blocks, Le Corbusier allowed himself the luxury of sculptural forms. They relate directly to his drawings and paintings, mixing Cubism with flowing shapes and vivid colors.*

5

4

6

7

5. Unité d'Habitation, Berlin, Germany *(1957). Le Corbusier. A third Unité (the second in Nantes, 1953) was built for the post-war Interbau exhibition. This model, backed up by Le Corbusier's own persuasive polemics, excited architects across the world. The result has spread worldwide.*

6. Carpenter Arts Center, Harvard, USA *(1964). Le Corbusier's last important building, while still assertive, is more sensitively modeled.*

7. Monastery of Sainte-Marie de la Tourette, Evreux, France *(1957-60). Le Corbusier. This large and severe Dominican monastery has a facade whose top story reflects the simple cell accommodation within. The austerity is appropriate to the Order, a moving tribute to an earlier medieval tradition.*

MIES VAN DER ROHE

1

2

1/2. Farnsworth House, Fox River, Illinois, USA (1950) *Mies van der Rohe. In this country pavilion, Mies expressed and concentrated every aspect of his genius into a simple rectangular volume of steel and glass. It is a classical house, Greek in subtlety and attention to detail, which floats serenely above its site on the eight columns which support roof and floor. A central core provides the bathroom, otherwise the plan is open, lightly screened into areas for sleeping and living. The walls of plate glass spill the interior into the surrounding trees. Furnishings are spare – not a house for the untidy.*

3. Seagram Building, New York (1956). *Mies van der Rohe, interiors by Philip Johnson. This bronze-clad slab was among the first of a new breed of skyscrapers to stand alone on its site. Most high-rise offices of the time stepped back as they rose to respect daylight requirements, but by isolating the tower in the center of its own piazza, the architects were able to achieve an uncluttered tower of great elegance.*

3

4

5

4. Federal Center, Chicago, USA *(1963). Mies van der Robe. In his quest for greater simplicity – his most famous maxim was "less is more" – Mies abandoned any attempt to give one story architectural precedence over another. Only the higher band around the top expresses the service floors, in this way isolating them from the lower offices.*

5. Johnson House, New Canaan, Connecticut, USA *(1949). Philip Johnson (b 1906). Although clearly inspired by Mies, Johnson created for himself an individual masterpiece in the genre of steel and glass. In a sense it is almost a non house, so transparent is its glass envelope that the visitor is never certain what is real and what reflection.*

6. Apartments, Lake Shore Drive, Chicago, USA *(1948-51). Mies van der Robe. Mies refused to allow balconies to these apartment buildings which he argued would betray their purity of form. Individual curtains were also banned: only standard metallic blinds were eventually permitted to screen these all-glass walls.*

6

EXPERIMENTS IN FORM & STRUCTURE

1

2

3

4

5

1. Eames House, Los Angeles, USA (1949). Charles Eames (1907-78). West Coast architecture has a spirit of its own; one of gaiety and elegance which must owe something to the climate. Eames, a distinguished furniture designer, built this house for himself out of industrial components. He incorporated movable screens so that he could vary the spatial volumes of the building.

2. Ford House, Aurora, Illinois, USA (1948). Bruce Goff (b 1904). Goff is an architect impossible to categorize. Like Frank Lloyd Wright, an early influence, his buildings are unpredictable, rarely continuing a theme or obsession stated in preceding buildings, but starting another. This umbrella house, constructed of surplus army components, is a typically idiosyncratic example.

3. Bavinger House, Norman, Oklahoma, USA (1957). Goff. One of the most extravagant of Goff's work, the Post-Modern Bavinger house is built as a spiral, with rooms suspended from a central rocky pylon. The romantic opposite to Miesian austerity.

4. Soleri House, Cave Creek, Arizona, USA (1951). Paolo Soleri (b 1919). Another visionary and highly personal architect, Soleri has sought to further the introduction of truly organic architecture, unfettered by traditional disciplines. He has produced many beautiful drawings for vast projects but his output is small. The desert house displays his love of sculptural, underground elements and rich textural finishes.

5. Norman House, Norman, Oklahoma, USA (1961). Herb Greene (b 1929). Continuing the theme of eccentric living, this prairie house must be considered some kind of culmination. Architecture here disintegrates into an intellectualized aesthetic of the shanty town.

CONCRETE FORMS

1

2   3

1. Kresge Auditorium, Cambridge, Massachusetts, USA *(1953-55). Eero Saarinen (1910-61). Saarinen's restless search for new form and structure is shown in this auditorium, spanned by a vast hyperbolic parabaloid roof].*

2. Yale University, Hockey Rink, Connecticut, USA *(1958). Saarinen. A massive serpentine concrete beam, sculpturally cantilevered and counter balanced each end, supports cables which carry and mold the cladding to this vast and whale-like roof.*

3. TWA Terminal, Kennedy Airport, New York *(1962). Saarinen felt that air terminals should reflect something of the excitement of air travel. His theory was superbly translated into this Expressionist building in shell concrete.*

4. Bandstand, Teotihuacan, Mexico *(1956). Felix Candela (b 1910). Born in Spain, Candela moved to Mexico after the Civil War. He soon built up a practice there and is the most famous exponent of shell concrete, usually incredibly delicate in section, but always mathematically analysed and sculpturally conceived.*

5. Restaurant, Xochimilco, Mexico *(1958). Candela. An astounding example of the extreme thinness of Candela's shells, resulting here in a structure of exceptional movement and grace. The steel reinforcing is overlaid with the smallest cover of high strength concrete, a cover rather thinner in the dry climate of Mexico than would be needed elsewhere.*

4

5

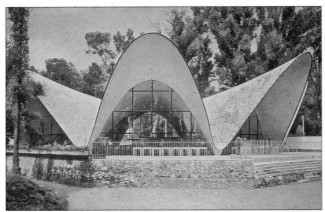

SCANDINAVIAN ARCHITECTS

1

1. Paimio Sanatorium, Finland (1929-33). Alvar Aalto (1898-1976). Aalto is a benign influence in twentieth-century architecture, bringing a welcome humanity into a movement all too often sterilized by intellectual theories. This early building, in which the wards are ranged in a long block to catch the sun, then a new concept, was revolutionary in both architectural and medical circles.

3

2

2. Forest Crematorium, Emskede, Stockholm, Sweden (1935-40). Gunnar Asplund (1885-1940). A disciple of William Morris, whose doctrines Asplund applied to the architecture and craft design of his own country, Sweden. In this way he almost single-handedly raised the standard of these arts to their present reputation. In these simple crematorium buildings, he created a classicism without orders or ornament, beautifully complementing the woodland background.

3. Sydney Opera House, Australia (1959-73). Jorn Utzon, Ove Arup and Hall, Todd & Littlemore. Utzon, a Danish pupil of Aalto's, won the Opera House commission in competition but resigned during its construction. In spite of its troubled history, the building, based on sail forms, retains most of its designer's original intentions with its controversial concrete shells.

4. Town Hall, Aarhus, Denmark (1938-42). Jacobsen & Møller. Jacobsen was the leading architect of his generation and this middle-period town hall shows his Scandinavian interpretation of the International Style at its most humane and competent.

4

5. Civic Center, Säynätsalo, Finland (1950-52). Aalto. In this group of public buildings, including the council chamber, offices, a library and shops, Aalto displayed his most successful integration of architecture with its landscape, carried out in beautifully detailed natural wood and roughly textured brickwork.

6. Finlandia Hall, Helsinki, Finland (1971). Aalto's last work, showing he had lost nothing of his touch in the handling of clean and expressive form. The building is clad entirely in white marble, adding to the crisp definition of surface and silhouette.

5

6

AMERICA IN THE 1960s

1. Marin County Civic Center, California, USA *(1959-62). Wright's last great work, completed after his death. Here his long-established love of horizontal form was concentrated to weld the building massively into the landscape. If it looks today like a space vehicle, this is because science fiction has borrowed from the architect, and not the other way around.*

2. Richards Research Building, Pennsylvania University, USA *(1960). Louis Kahn (1902-74). Kahn made a comparatively late entry on the international scene but became celebrated as both designer and teacher. His love of towers, inspired by a visit to the medieval town of San Geminiano in Italy, became a feature in all his work. At times he rationalized this by a contrived division into "served" and "servant" elements, which gave him the excuse to incorporate dramatic vertical shafts.*

3. Foreign Office, Brasilia, Brazil *(1962-70). Oscar Niemeyer (b 1907). This majestic building in the new capital city, Brasilia, shows Niemeyer in an unusually restrained, even classical, mood. A strong adherent of Le Corbusier, his employment of form is usually more romantic, even Expressionist.*

4. Salk Institute, La Jolla, California, USA *(1963-65). Kahn. A severe but interestingly modeled group of buildings, reminiscent of Le Corbusier in its treatment of concrete. More subtle in detailing than may appear at first glance.*

2

3

4

1

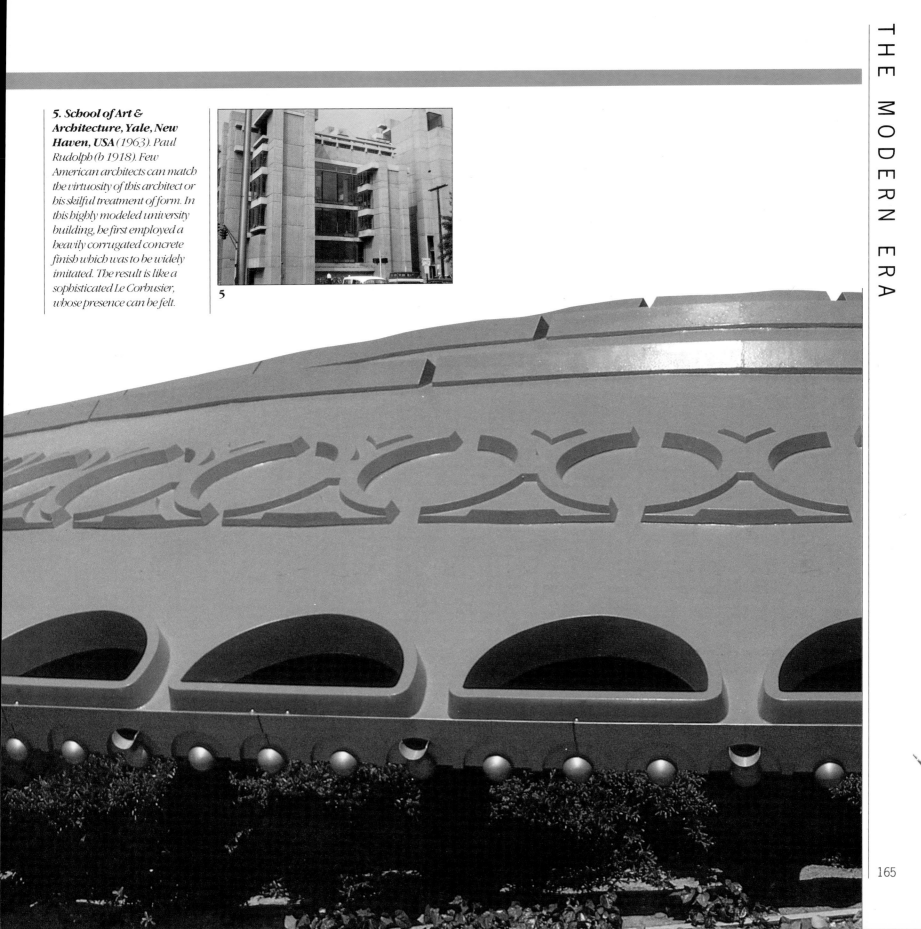

5. School of Art & Architecture, Yale, New Haven, USA *(1963). Paul Rudolph (b 1918). Few American architects can match the virtuosity of this architect or his skilful treatment of form. In this highly modeled university building, he first employed a heavily corrugated concrete finish which was to be widely imitated. The result is like a sophisticated Le Corbusier, whose presence can be felt.*

5

AMERICA IN THE 1960s

1

2

3

1. City Hall, Boston, USA *(1962-69). Kallman, McKinnel & Knowles. This remarkable competition winner has elements of Le Corbusier and his disciples in post-war Japan. The concrete here is less brutally exposed and the composition, while asymmetrical, wears a classical air.*

2. Apartment Building, Cambridge, USA *(1964). Sert, Jackson & Gourlay. Sert was born in Spain and later worked for Le Corbusier whose influence can be felt in these apartment buildings. Equally accomplished at city planning or designing small houses, Sert is explicit and unpretentious.*

3. Church, Columbus, Indiana, USA *(1964). Saarinen. Until his comparatively early death, Saarinen created an extraordinary variety of highly sculptural buildings, each one seemingly representing a fresh approach, almost as if by a different hand. This lively architect is well represented by this church, completed after his premature death.*

4. Marina City, Chicago, USA *(1964-68). Bertrand Goldberg Associates. These circular towers bring a welcome relief to the hard background of towers and slabs. An ingenious solution to high-rise luxury housing.*

5. John Hancock Center, Chicago, USA *(1966-68). Skidmore, Owings & Merrill. The famous firm was associated with clean solutions of immaculately detailed curtain walling. In the sixties, however, an element of Mannerism crept in, as in this Chicago tower where structural bracing is openly expressed up and down the facade.*

6. Lake Point Tower, Chicago, USA *(1968). Schipporeit & Heinrich Inc. An interesting counterpoint to the Mies apartments on Lake Shore Drive. Perhaps a reaction to the simple block was inevitable, and this tower is interestingly comparable to early but unbuilt Mies' designs. New technology here incorporates bronze glass to mitigate the fierce summer.*

EUROPE IN THE 50s & 60s

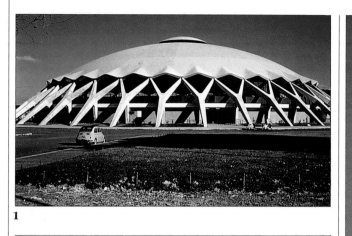

1

2

3

1. Palazzetto dello Sport, Rome (1959). Nervi. One of the two magnificent stadia built for the Olympics by Italy's foremost engineer. The lively concrete Y-frame structure is dramatic.

2. Hunstanton School, Norfolk, England (1954). Smithsons. The introduction of "New Brutalism" came when the Smithsons won this school in competition. All building elements and services were openly expressed, an approach predating the "Boilerhouse" school of the seventies.

3. Pirelli Building, Milan, Italy (1955-58). Gio Ponti (1891-1979). An elegant tower by one of Italy's most sophisticated artists, equally accomplished as a furniture designer and painter. The tapered profile was made possible by a structural core of reinforced concrete by Nervi.

4. Philharmonie, Berlin, Germany *(1956-63). Hans Scharoun (1893-1972). The exterior of this curious building shows little of the spatial coherence, however wayward, of the interior. In Scharoun, the battle between the Expressionist and the Classical Modernist never appears to have been entirely resolved but his dedication is impressive.*

4

5

5. Engineering Faculty, Leicester, England *(1964). Stirling & Gowan. Another source of New Brutalism was introduced by this partnership. After this sculptured block at Leicester, the architects went their independent ways. The Mannerism which can now be detected in Stirling's work is evident here in the treatment of the cantilevered forms.*

MODERNISM IN THE EAST

1

1. Viceroy's House, Delhi, India *(1913-27). Sir Edwin Lutyens (1869-1944). Commissions for the state capital at Delhi brought Lutyens' career to its imperial climax. Classical grammar, here wittily affecting an Indian accent, underlies all his work, which is nevertheless highly personal and underivative.*

2

2. Olympic Pool, Tokyo, Japan. *(1964). Kenzo Tange (b 1913). A brilliant sports building by the outstanding genius of modern Japanese architecture. Early influence from Le Corbusier weakened as Tange moved further into a sculptured Expressionism.*

3. St Mary's Roman Catholic Cathedral, Tokyo, Japan *(1965). Tange twisted metal-sheathed concrete walls as if they were paper in huge curvilinear planes where they converge in a cruciform plan at the center. The result is simple, bold and magnificent.*

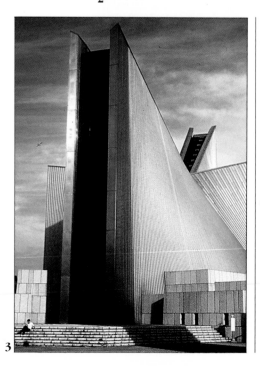

3

4

5

4. Delegates Hostel, Dacca, Bangladesh *(1962-74). Kahn. In 1962, Kahn was invited to produce a master plan and buildings for new government architecture at Dacca. The Mannerist geometry of his mature style is here economically translated into massive brickwork.*

5. Art Museum, Kitakyushu, Japan *(1972). Arata Isozaki (b 1931). A fondness for wildly cantilevered block forms is a feature of much Japanese architecture. Here it is expressed in its most exaggerated form where these cantilevers are poised like twin barrels on some gun emplacement.*

1. World Trade Center, New York *(1962-77). Yamasaki & Roth. These famous twin towers now dominate lower Manhattan, impressive by their size and by the magical way they catch the low sun of dawn and sunset. Architecturally they border on the dull and become oppressive close to.*

2. Hancock Tower, Boston, USA *(1973). I.M. Pei (b 1917). This award-winning colossal glass slab ran into trouble when glazing panels started to blow off in gales. Architecturally it takes the aesthetic of the glass tower to new and astounding heights.*

3. National Gallery, Washington DC, USA *(1978). Pei. A difficult triangular site on which to build this gallery extension. Pei solved the problem brilliantly with this simple but sculptural wedge.*

4. Gehry Residence, Los Angeles, USA *(1977). Frank Gehry (b 1929). The playfulness of recent architecture seems prominent in this wilfully inappropriate, but clearly intentional remodeling of an ordinary surburban house.*

5. Pennzoil Place, Houston, Texas, USA *(1976). Johnson & Burgee. An exceptionally sophisticated essay by Johnson, one of the world's most polished architects. The tension between the blocks is intensified by the distortion of perspective caused by sloping rooflines and inclined planes.*

3

4

5

BRITAIN IN THE 1970s

1. Cumbernauld New Town, Strathclyde, Scotland (1956). A post-Corbusier shopping center reflecting some of the virtues and faults of Brutalist concrete. At present largely discredited, the ultimate status of this school has yet to be established. The town serves to house Glasgow's commuter population and is divided up into villages.

1

3

2. IBM offices, Havant, England (1970). Foster Associates. The sophisticated packaging of these offices takes the Mies-Johnson glass building into the commercial field. Success depends, as here, on immaculate attention to detail and constant maintenance.

3. Willis Faber & Dumas Offices, Ipswich, England (1975). Foster Associates. During the day, the external dark glass walls, molded to the profile of an irregular site, reflect the street facades opposite – an exciting if disturbing experience. By night the facade dissolves to reveal the three-story, illuminated interior.

4. Byker Housing, Newcastle, England (1970-80). Ralph Erskine (b 1914). A vast housing scheme for 10,000 people commissioned by Newcastle Council, in which colorful blocks are linked in curved and irregular terraces. In spite of their individuality, the influence of Erskine's adopted country of Sweden is clear, though none the worse for that. The project was unique in strong tenant participation at every stage.

AMERICAN POST MODERNISM

1

1. Chestnut Hill, Philadelphia, USA (1962-64). Robert Venturi (b 1925). In this house, which Venturi built for his mother, he broke the mold of Modernism, creating, with others, the movement which has come to be known as Post-Modernism. More simply, it represents a reaction against the severe geometry of previous twentieth-century styles.

2/3. Loyola Law School, Los Angeles, USA (1981). Frank Gehry & Associates. Classical forms are here reduced and splintered into children's building blocks, whose wit disguises the underlying seriousness. Nevertheless, the effect is at once both disquieting and entertaining.

A street view of the school shows the chapel; the building on the left is part of the old complex. The skylight to the chapel fails to respect the geometry of the roof – a deliberate, if uncomfortable mannerism.

2

3

4

4. Public Services Building, Portland, Oregon, USA

(1982). Michael Graves (b 1934). Decoration made a return to architecture after years of aesthetic doldrums, in this case apparently in homage to thirties cinema style. It is hard to know whether architecture, like many other serious arts, has become a kind of sophisticated joke, but if so, on whom does the joke fall?

A garland, in which a Neo-Classical motif has been reduced to cartoon status, is reminiscent of contemporary schools in painting, which derive from commercial art and illustration.

5. 2-4-6-8 House, Los Angeles, USA

(1979). Morphosis Architects. This jolly house uses traditional Cubist forms with color and texture.

6. House at New Castle, Delaware, USA

(1978). Venturi has used cut-out early Doric or Cretan columns as symbolic substitutes for genuine structural members, brutally amputating one side just in case it might be misconstrued. The ambiguity and metaphor is both calculated and serious.

5

6

1. Les Arenes de Picasso, Marne-la-Vallée, Paris (1984). Nunez-Yanowsky. A housing development on the outskirts of Paris; unlike other European cities, the satellite towns around Paris are experimental and bold.

2. Palace of Abraxas, Marne-la-Vallée, France (1978-82). Bofill & Taller de Arquitectura. The Spanish architect Ricardo Bofill made a dramatic and monumental entrance into the architectural arena. His housing with massively constructed Classical forms recalls the pre-war fascist architecture of Mussolini and Hitler, overlaid with Post-Modern clichés and Art Deco styling.

3. Staats Galerie, Stuttgart, Germany (1984). James Stirling & Wilford Associates. Color and textural variety are features of recent Stirling buildings. His continuing dexterity and control of spatial elements has been sweetened by an increasing harmony of surface and slightly self-consious sculptural elements.

4. Cement Works, Barcelona, Spain (1975). Bofill can create monumentalism out of anything. These impressive abstract forms of a cement works became, in his hands, a medieval fortress. The grass and cypresses add an incongruous but magical touch.

2

3

4

5

6

5. Public Library, San Juan, California, USA (1983). Graves. Strong West Coast sunlight accentuates the sculptural shapes of this Post-Modern library gateway, whose open lattice canopy provides style and shadow, if not shelter.

6. Clore Gallery, London (1987). James Stirling & Wilford Associates. Stirling was commissioned to build the new wing onto the Tate Gallery to house the works of J.M.W. Turner. The linking wing is architecturally neutral, in deference to the Neo-Renaissance of the older gallery. It gradually blossoms into the openly Expressionist architecture of the principal block.

BOILERHOUSE ARCHITECTURE

1

2 3

4

1. Renault Distribution Center, Swindon, England (1965). Foster Associates. Norman Foster has developed one of the most successful commercial practices in the UK, combining a flair for detailing with exciting technology. Both are clearly present in this industrial example.

2. Sainsbury Center for the Visual Arts, Norwich, England (1977). Foster Associates. Foster conceived this gallery as a vast hangar in an open field site. The night view shows the essentially simple space and industrial structure.

3. Pompidou Center, Paris (1972-77). Piano & Rogers. The competition brief was for large uninterrupted spaces for exhibitions and displays, multi story to satisfy the site restrictions of a busy street. The answer was this striking structure in which all the elements of engineering and services are ruthlessly exposed. The snaky tube climbing the outside, houses an escalator.

4. Lloyds Building, London (1986). Richard Rogers (b 1933). Rogers created this inside-out, technological framework in the new Lloyds building. This controversial building is basically a large atrium around which the services, elevators and staircases – traditionally placed inside a building – are externally expressed.

5/6. Hong Kong Shanghai Bank, Hong Kong (1981-85). Foster Associates. Foster is never architecturally incoherent and his technological bias is always classically handled. In this vast skyscraper, the vertebrate skeleton is boldly and effectively exposed, giving great visual and structural confidence. Inside, the central court is like a power house whose immense scale can be judged by the figure on the bridge. Functionally this provides a cool air-conditioned atrium against the sub-tropical summers.

6

5

2

1. Casa Rotunda, Stabio, Switzerland *(1981).*
Mario Botta. Hardly a house for the domestic. Botta has used simple forms to create a stern and uncompromising statement, one in which the client will have to make the concessions.

2. Anderson Building, Los Angeles County Museum of Art, California, USA *(1986).*
N. Pfeiffer. One curious manifestation of Post Modernism is delight in surface decoration, rather like stylized camouflage. Would Ruskin or Morris have approved of such arbitrary and structurally detached ornamentation?

3. Crystal Cathedral, Garden Grove, California, USA *(1980). Johnson. A cathedral of a different kind. Johnson first experimented with the reflective qualities of glass to mirror – imperfectly – the surrounding buildings. The interior is like a gigantic greenhouse turned on its end.*

3

1

4

4. Aerospace Museum, Los Angeles, USA (1984). Gehry. This lively building seems most appropriate for its function. The West Coast Spirit, with its freedom and money, asserts itself in an enjoyable architecture.

BACK TO TRADITION

4

1. Portmeirion, Gwynedd, Wales (1933-72). Clough Williams Ellis (d 1978). Ellis is a maverick figure in twentieth-century architecture. His formal training was minimal, but he survived on his passion for old buildings, combined with an inheritance which allowed him the freedom to develop this picturesque bay in Wales into a Mediterranean port, akin to Portofino in Italy. This was started before the restrictions of planning committees. The result is architecturally eclectic, structurally meager, aesthetically theatrical and wholly enjoyable. The site was added to right up to Ellis' death from his incomparable stock of architectural salvage. For this commitment, he deserves our gratitude.

2. Liverpool Anglican Cathedral, England (1903-78). Giles Gilbert Scott (1880-1960). Lutyens had designed a huge domed Catholic cathedral for Liverpool but World War II prevented more than the completion of its crypt. Scott was more fortunate; his less ambitious Anglican Cathedral, won in competition, was finally completed to his design after his death. Some may find its austere Gothic to be an anachronism in the twentieth century but its admirers believe it to be the finest work of its kind since John Pearson's Truro Cathedral (1879-1910). Whatever the style, what impresses is the authority and professionalism of its composition and detailing. Its tower has given Liverpool a magnificent addition to its skyline.

3. Old Bailey Extension, London (1972). McMorran & Whitby. The Neo-Baroque criminal court (1900) was extended in 1972 and excited much interest and admiration from supporters of traditional architecture. It differs from most post-war Neo-Georgian in that the architects took a fresh and tough-minded look at classical vocabulary and produced a city facade which is an original and eloquent interpretation of the functions of the building.

4. House, Sydney, Australia (1980). Glenn Murcutt (b 1936). An attempt at a vernacular style. This house reflects a deliberate return to the simple timber frame and corrugated iron buildings of the Australian outback.

GLOSSARY

Abacus The flat piece at the top of a *capital*.

Acropolis A Greek citadel containing temples, usually situated on the highest point overlooking a city.

Agora Greek market place.

Aisle An area in a church parallel to the *nave*.

Ambulatory An *aisle* in a circular or semicircular building; frequently at the east end of a cathedral or large church.

Apse A recess, often semicircular, usually found on the end wall in the chapel.

Arcade Arches on *piers* or *columns,* either standing on their own or part of a wall.

Architrave The lowest part of the *entablature*.

Atrium An inner courtyard in a Roman house.

Balcony A platform that extends from a wall.

Baldacchino A *canopy* that stands over a throne or altar.

Baptistery Part of a church that contains a font for baptism.

Baroque A style that is whimsical and with masses of decoration, particularly seventeenth-century Italy.

Barrel vault The simplest form of *vault,* a semicircular, continuous section.

Basilica In Roman architecture a meeting hall; the layout was used for Early Christian houses of worship. Essential characteristics were an oblong plan, timber roof and *apse*.

Bauhaus School of Arts founded in 1906 using progressive workshop-based teaching methods, with all areas of the arts working together.

Bay The spaces in a building marked out by the windows, *columns* etc.

Beaux Arts The leading French Academy of fine art.

Brutalism School describing Le Corbusier's work (especially Unité d'Habitation) and others who followed (Stirling). Exposed materials such as concrete without dressing it up.

Buttress A solid wall support made of brick or stone.

Campanile A bell tower in Italian, usually freestanding.

Canopy A projection over a window, altar, door.

Cantilever A structural part of a building that extends horizontally beyond its obvious means of support.

Capital The top of a *column* or *pilaster,* usually decorated.

Caryatid A *column* carved as a female figure.

Chancel At the east end of a church where the choir and main altar are situated; reserved for the clergy.

Chantry chapel A chapel within a church endowed for the soul of the benefactor.

Chevron A zigzag-shaped *moulding (Romanesque).*

Chicago School Architects such as Sullivan working in Chicago at the end of the nineteenth century, responsible for the early *skyscrapers*.

Choir Part of a church where the singing takes place.

Circus In Roman times, a long building with tiered seating and rounded ends.

Classicism (Classical) Styles that use Greek or Roman architecture as the established principles.

Clerestory A wall above the roof of the *aisle* containing windows.

Clocher The French word for a bell tower.

Cloisters The connecting corridor between a monastery and the monk's quarters, usually roofed and vaulted.

Colonnade Row of *columns*.

Column A cylindrical support, sometimes tapering, consisting usually of a base, shaft and *capital.* The top part is the *entablature*.

Corinthian The most ornate of the *Classical orders.*

Cornice The projecting ornamental *moulding* at the top of the *entablature* or along a wall or arch.

Cupola A *dome,* usually small.

Curtain wall A freestanding wall in front of the main frame of a building, usually glass. Originally the outer fortified wall of a castle.

Diaper work Surface decoration, usually in small repeated patterns.

Dome A *vault* on a circular base forming part of a sphere.

Donjon A French word for a castle stronghold or *keep*.

Doric order Simplest of the *Classical orders.*

Drum A circular or polygonal wall that supports a *dome*.

Eaves The underneath part of a sloping roof that overhangs a wall.

Elevation The vertical plane of a building; sometimes a drawing showing the exterior.

Entablature The upper part of a *Classical order*.

Fan vault A *vault* in which the *ribs* spread out like a fan.

Fenestration The windows in a building and their arrangement.

Flying buttress An external *buttress* built to take lateral forces from roof vaults by means of intermediate arches.

Folly A structure with no purpose, showing the "folly" of the owner.

Forum An open assembling point surrounded by buildings and *colonnades*.

Frieze A decorated band on an *entablature*.

Gable Triangular part of the wall at the ridge of the roof.

Gallery In a church the upper floor over the *aisle* looking down upon the *nave*. A narrow room in a house.

Gothic The pointed arch is the most obvious characteristic of this style of architecture dating from the twelfth century.

Greek cross A cross with four equal arms; the basis for Greek church layouts.

Groin The sharp edge where two *vaults* intersect.

Half-timbered A building with a timber frame and infill or nogging in between.

Harled Another term for *rough casting,* e.g. pebbledashed.

Hyperbolic paraboloid roof A curved structural shape in which, in concrete construction, all reinforcing can be laid in straight lines.

Insula An apartment building in ancient Rome.

Ionic One of the *Classical orders*.

International Modern A term used to describe architecture before the First World War of such architects as Loos and Gropius. Includes white rendering, horizontal glazing, cubed shape.

Keep The inner stronghold in a castle containing the quarters to provide accommodation during a siege.

Lancet Simple, thin, pointed *Gothic* window, typical of Early English style.

Lantern A windowed tower on top of a *dome*.

Layout The building on plan.

Loggia A *gallery,* open along one side, sometimes with *columns*.

Madrassa An Islamic theological college or *mosque*.

Mannerism Refers to a style in Italy during the time of Michelangelo when motifs were used in precisely the opposite context to that which was normally accepted. Figures were contorted. Now the word refers to the manner in which something is done rather than the meaning behind it.

Mansard roof A roof with two sloping sections; the lower is more steeply sloped than the upper.

Mason A builder who works with stone.

Minaret A tall tower associated with a *mosque*. The *balconies* are where the call to prayer is made.

Modulor A system set down by Le Corbusier in his work of 1951, *Le Modulor,* in which the male body was used to establish the proportions of building spaces.

Mosque A Moslem place of worship.

Mouldings Ornamental projections such as beading, *diaper work, chevrons* etc.

Naos A place in a Greek temple where the statue of the god was kept; the sanctuary.

Nave. The main body of a church bordered by the *aisles*.

Orangery An early conservatory – a glazed building in which oranges were grown.

Order The design of a *column* and its *entablature.*

Oriels A curved projecting window on an upper *story.*

Parapet A low wall placed near a sudden drop such as on a roof or bridge.

Pavilion A summerhouse or part of a more substantial building, usually of light construction.

Pendentive Means by which a circular *dome* is supported above a rectangular space. Triangle-like overhanging shapes at the corners.

Pedestal The base that supports a *column.*

Pediment The triangular-shaped *gable* above a window or door, or a *Classical* end treatment to the triangle formed by a gate.

Peristyle *Columns* that surround a courtyard or a building.

Perpendicular style Derived from the classification of the window *tracery* with vertical and horizontal divisions. Used to describe medieval architecture in England.

Piano nobile The main floor of an Italian Renaissance villa, usually raised above a basement providing the main living quarters.

Piazza Public area, surrounded by buildings.

Pier A support, not as slender as a *column,* made of solid masonry.

Pilaster A rectangular *column* that conforms with one of the *orders* and projects from a wall.

Pillar A support that does not conform to the *Classical orders.*

Pilotis Stilts or pillars that support a building, raising it above the ground; used by Le Corbusier.

Plinth The projecting base, either of a wall or a *column.*

Portico A porch or covered entrance area, sometimes surrounded by a *colonnade.*

Post Modern More a spirit than a style, this has emerged in the last 20 years. Exponents include Venturi, Graves and Stirling.

Precast concrete Components are cast and molded at a factory and then placed in position.

Pylon Ancient Egyptian towers that flank the entrance (to a temple). Now used for a structure shaped this way and marking a boundary.

Reinforced concrete Concrete strengthened by the insertion of steel rods.

Rendering Plaster covering an external surface.

Rib A projecting band across a ceiling or on a *groin,* usually structural.

Rib vault A *groin vault* in which the *ribs* cross on the diagonal.

Ridge The junction of two slopes on a roof.

Rococo Last phase of the *Baroque* with ornamental decoration that was light and often naturalistic.

Romanesque The rounded arch is the basis for this style, variously dated at between the seventh and tenth century.

Rose window A round window with *tracery* and stained glass radiating out like the spokes of a wheel.

Rotunda A round room or building.

Roughcast An outer coating of a rough material e.g. pebbledash.

Rusticated column A *column* in which rough blocks have been introduced down its length.

Saracenic Of the Saracen or Islamic style.

Skyscraper A building constructed on a steel skeleton making greater height possible. Origin in the USA in the 1880s with the *Chicago School.*

Spandrel Triangular space between an arch and a wall or between two arches.

Spire A tall pointed structure rising from a tower on the roof, usually of a church.

Stalactite work Ornamental brickwork in Islamic architecture, found on the ceiling.

Steeple The *spire* and tower of a church taken together.

Stepped gable A *gable* with stepped sides, originally in Holland.

Stoa A detached *colonnade* in Greek architecture.

Story The space between two floors. In this country the story at ground level is called the first floor, in Europe it is called the ground floor.

Strapwork Decoration found in Elizabethan England and Holland where the work is rather like cut leather. Used on ceilings and screens.

Stucco A plaster covering.

Thermae Public baths (Roman).

Tholos A circular building with *dome.*

Tracery Ornamental stone framework.

Transept The transverse arms of a cross-shaped church.

Triforium The middle *story* of a church or cathedral, usually in the form of a simple *gallery,* often in blind arcading.

Trusses Structural members, usually supporting roofs, made up of independent members joined together to form a whole.

Turret A slender tower.

Vault An arched ceiling or roof, usually brick or stone.

Volute A spiral scroll, found on an *Ionic capital.*

INDEX

GENERAL INDEX

Page numbers in **bold** refer to illustrations

INDEX